WOMEN OF SPIRIT

To my family and friends—and especially to my new family and new friends, among whom I am delighted to discover more women of Spirit.

Women of Spirit

Compiled by

Dorothy Stewart

A LION BOOK

This collection, with biographies, copyright © 1997 Dorothy Stewart.
All quotations from living authors and those who died less than fifty years ago
are copyright and are included by permission (see separate Acknowledgments).

The author asserts the moral right
to be identified as the author of this work

Published by
Lion Publishing plc
Sandy Lane West, Oxford, England
ISBN 0 7459 3671 7
Albatross Books Pty Ltd
PO Box 320, Sutherland, NSW 2232, Australia
ISBN 0 7324 1506 3

First edition 1997
10 9 8 7 6 5 4 3 2 1 0

A catalogue record for this book is available
from the British Library

Printed and bound in Great Britain
by Cox and Wyman Ltd, Reading

Contents

LEARNING TO GROW

FACING THE FACTS

PART TWO: REAL LIVES, REAL PAIN

NO INSURANCE POLICY—ONLY GRACE

PART THREE: THE REAL WORLD

THE CALL TO ACTION

PART FOUR: TIME TO REJOICE

Introduction

Women of Spirit seems to follow on quite naturally from *Women of Prayer* (published by Lion in 1993). So many of the prayers I discovered had been spoken or written by women who were both spirited and spiritual and I wanted the opportunity to share some more of what they had to say. So, yes, the pun is deliberate. This is a collection of writings by women who are inspired by God's Spirit and who have spirited natures—as thinkers, preachers, writers, doctors, teachers, mums, wives, friends... the whole gamut of womankind. Because, after all, the God who made us in Her image, made us that way!

I have learnt much from these women. They hold a mirror up, showing who we are and who we might become. And so I hope their writings will offer inspiration and encouragement. They are us—sometimes more so, sometimes less so. But they are us.

What I have learned is that women of Spirit know that they need God and they take time and space to draw near to him. They use lots of different ways—some prefer to chat to their Heavenly Father, almost like having a friendly phone-call home. Others choose the way of silence. All take time to listen for God's answer, whether through their prayer or Bible-reading, or through sensitivity to God's messages via other people or the world around them.

They aren't perfect. These women know their shortcomings—their bad temper, impatience, lack of humility, whatever it is. They face the sin and failure in their lives—and by offering it openly to God, they enable him to transform it and them.

They suffer. The tragedies and miseries of life do not

13

pass them by. Not all are heroines like Aida of Leningrad, imprisoned for her faith, but all have some experience to offer common to the general lot of women—illness, operations, pain, death of friends and relatives, their own death. And as they face these courageously or with honest fear, they reveal the resources of God's Spirit on which they draw.

They care about the world they live in. They have a vision which begins with their own fireside and takes in the whole world. Here are politics, revolution, militant Christianity. Here is challenge.

Whatever else they may be, they are real women, mainly of our own century, mostly still alive, still working out their salvation as God's Spirit enables them. They juggle real lives, just like the rest of us—the concerns and constraints of families, whether elderly relatives, young children or friends, the daily requirements of work, inside and outside the home, church activities, social lives, and all the rest. Most of these women are Western women like me—their stories rang bells with me and I hope they will chime with you.

You will find words of inspiration, of comfort, encouragement and challenge. But most of all, you will hear the words of women who are prepared to let God's Spirit into their lives in all the reality that is life today.

PART ONE

Keep close to God

Women of Spirit keep close to God. Most pray. Some chat in friendly terms, some sit in silence. Some read their Bible, some watch birds! All consider the time spent with their Heavenly Father as pivotal in their lives. It is from this space that they find the resources they need for their life and their work, and their growth as children of God. And they recognize that growth as needing application and dedication, just as in any garden. As one writer says, we need to keep the path clear!

But paths can easily become overgrown with weeds and so, too, do lives fall into sin and failure. Women of Spirit are honest about their failings, recognizing the masks we all hide behind—and take them to God.

There is an assurance, a freedom here to be who you are, and become who God wants you to be—fulfilled, filled with joy and His Spirit.

Let us pray

Only one prayer

There is really only one possible prayer: Give me to do everything I do in the day with a sense of the sacredness of life. Give me to be in Your presence, God, even though I know it only as absence.

MAY SARTON

Our part

We are only syllables of the perfect Word.

CARYLL HOUSELANDER

Letting go

I finally decided that I must give up stating the case in my prayers, and telling God what I thought He ought to do, and instead just kneel down before God, and put [it] before Him simply by saying [a] name… like the old peasant who had a bad foot, but since he did not know which was best for him, to be cured, to be lame, to be in pain or out of pain, he just went to church and said, 'Lord—foot'.

CARYLL HOUSELANDER

Letting God

In the beginning of my sobriety, for instance, I had no idea what 'let go and let God' meant. It's only five words, and I understand it very well today, but at that time, I was directing God, telling Him what *I* wanted. I probably gave Him a list.

BETTY FORD

Don't give up

Sustained efforts are necessary. If you spend your time pulling down with one hand what you build up with the other, you will never achieve anything. This is not the work of a day but a lifetime, so it is no use just making one or two isolated efforts; you have to persevere. Remember what the Apocalypse says: 'Be thou faithful *unto death* and I will give thee the crown of life.' Nothing can be had for nothing. The kingdom of God suffereth violence. And what about you? You don't mind making a few attempts, but to keep the effort up costs too much altogether!

JULIE BILLIART

Remove the mask

A Christian's relationship with God is just as stormy and precarious as any human relationship. It is just as hard to remove your mask and open up to God as it is to those around you and the fear of rejection is more intense because it is an infinite, eternal, ultimate rejection. I will argue… that this fear is groundless. It arises mainly because, I feel, we read too much of ourselves into God.

ELIZABETH STUART

Like a child to her father

The simple person goes straight to God like a child to her father... It is easy for her to draw near to him for she is so direct in her prayer, and God on his side loves to talk with one who is as candid and simple as a child.

JULIE BILLIART

Eyes shut or eyes open?

Some people find it easier than others to sustain a personal relationship with God through prayer... Prayer can, however, become a mere symptom of our brokenness. It is easy to use prayer to try to impose upon God our own desires, concerns and opinions and to justify our alienated condition. We avoid the guilt and frustration of facing our shared responsibility for most of the misery in the world by turning in upon ourselves and concerning ourselves only with our own salvation. When we hear the words 'Let us pray' what do most of us do? We bow our heads, close our eyes, perhaps kneel down, and immediately start to think about our own needs and pet causes. We turn in upon ourselves and we set the agenda. We are afraid to let God in in case he shows us something or someone we do not want to see and calls us into situations we would rather avoid. A person who is seeking wholeness and has a desire to communicate God's grace to others will, metaphorically at least, pray with their eyes open, to allow God to direct their eyes towards what forms their shadow side, in need of love and acceptance, and also towards people and situations calling for his healing grace.

ELIZABETH STUART

Pray with your whole heart

Prayer is naught else but a yearning of soul... when it is practised with the whole heart, it has great power. It makes a sour heart sweet, a sad heart merry, a poor heart rich, a foolish heart wise, a timid heart courageous, a sick heart well, a blind heart full of vision, a cold heart ardent. For it draws down the great God into the little heart; it drives the hungry soul up to the plenitude of God; it brings together these two lovers, God and the soul, in a wondrous place where they speak much of love.

MECHTHILD OF MAGDEBURG

Where shall I find God?

Where shall I find God? In myself. That is the true Mystical Doctrine. But then I myself must be in a state for Him to come and dwell in me. This is the whole aim of the Mystical life; and all Mystical rules in all time and countries have been laid down for putting the soul into such a state...

FLORENCE NIGHTINGALE

Don't hang up—hang on

Waiting for the answer

It is during our busy, noisy times when we rush about, making as much noise as we can, that things go wrong. We do not stop to think, let alone tackle problems.

When we want advice from anyone and telephone to ask for it, do we quickly tell them what our difficulty is and then hang up the receiver before getting a reply? That is our usual attitude when we ask God for help. We hang up quickly and start rushing about again, instead of being quiet and waiting for a reply.

It is in the quietness that we shall get some sort of answer and peace of mind. This is a difficult thing to do at times, but it will come with practice if we can start now. Every time we talk to God we should take a few minutes and listen inwardly.

VICTORIA LIDIARD

God still speaks

The one idea he did leave with me was that God could speak to me. That really intrigued me, for I had often wondered when God stopped speaking to people, as he seemed to have done in the Bible, with the saints, even with my namesake and heroine, Joan of Arc. The next morning, I decided to make an experiment. I would ask the God I believed in, but was sure took no interest in me, to speak to me. If any thought came that could conceivably be construed as coming from God, I would take it seriously and act on it. It worked. Actually, the only thought that came was a text—I suppose I had such a narrow idea of God that I thought he would speak in texts. But what struck me most was that the text happened to be 'Be still and know that I am God.'

I knew my Bible pretty well so any number of other verses could have come into my mind. I found it at least interesting that a verse saying what I so much wanted to hear should be the one that came to me. Then another odd thing happened. My temper was always, to say the least, quickly aroused. That morning, almost as soon as I got downstairs, something happened to cross my will and my temper flared. But at once that text slipped into my mind—and my temper vanished! I remember standing there by the dining-room table thinking 'That's a miracle!'

From then on I began to put aside a short time each morning in which to be quiet.

JOAN PORTER BUXTON

Practising the presence of God

The only way I can learn it [the practice of the presence of God] is to do it, and one thing I am very sure of for myself is that to sit quietly before God doing nothing, only fixing the will gently on some expressive word like 'O God, I want Thee' or 'Father' or 'Here am I and here are You' makes a world of difference. Just as laying in the sun doing nothing, surrendering your body to it, with the sun blazing down on you, affects your body and your senses, so this surrendering of the soul to that transforming Power affects the soul, and I believe that as truly as the sun changes the colour of your skin so that Power changes you at the centre.

FLORENCE ALLSHORN

Staying awake

Increasingly, prayer seems to be a waiting—and often, a goal-less waiting: it is simply an end in itself. If some resolution, insight or peace comes, it comes as a gift, not as something I have angled for. I was at a loss to explain this to anyone until I remembered that the French for 'to wait' is 'attendre'. Then it became clear that waiting is giving one's complete and undivided attention… to the present moment, to the person or situation one wants to 'hold in the Light', to the object before one's eyes, or the word arising in one's mind. To keep vigil is to be awake, waiting, attentive.

KATE COMPSTON

Silence

[One] who neglects silence brings only a distracted heart and a preoccupied mind to her prayer and, instead of deriving new strength from it, she only makes herself guilty before God by going to him with a heart taken up by trifles... Intimate conversation with God is easily stifled if you do not first put an end to exterior chatter; but if you love silence and keep it well, your heart will be a temple where God will dwell. He will make his will known to you there. He will receive your constant adoration and will converse familiarly with you.

JULIE BILLIART

In the dark

I no longer panic at dry or so-called dark periods... I learned long ago that if those times didn't come, we wouldn't be normal. How we feel—how I *feel* 'spiritually'—seems less and less relevant. What matters is that God is *constant*. He is the *only* constant anywhere in the world.

EUGENIA PRICE

Clinging to God

It is good to have some desolation in prayer, it makes us cling to God.

JULIE BILLIART

Trust—like a cat

No sooner had he [her cat, Jones] jumped on my lap than he relaxed, he went limp... happily, deliciously limp and indicated by various signs known to me that he wanted his ears scratched—that done, he went to sleep. I ought to be able to treat God as my cat treats me, only, whereas my cat is deluded about my omnipotence, I am right about God's.

CARYLL HOUSELANDER

God keeps his promises

A verse from the book of Proverbs says, 'God keeps every promise he makes.' I have found in my life, in every circumstance, that this is true. He has never disappointed me, and the nearer I get to him, the deeper I enter into his life, then I find his promises unfolding like leaves in spring, and there at the centre the kernel which is His everlasting love—His promise fulfilled in me and for me. Draw closer to Him now. You will not be disappointed. The closer you come, the more you will be able to receive, and the more you will have to share.

MARGARET CUNDIFF

Being God's friend

I've caught on, I think, to something of what St Paul meant when he wrote that we were to 'pray without ceasing'. My devotional times are not as 'scheduled' as they once were, but then I was knocking myself out trying to be a 'good and faithful servant'. You see, I've learned that He [Jesus] meant it when he said that He would no longer call His disciples servants, but *friends*. I have a very simple goal now: to be God's friend.

EUGENIA PRICE

Offertory and consecration

I am the cold insipid water ready to be poured
into the chalice.
Let me be put into the wine like the drop of water
at this Mass.
Let me be flooded through with the strength, the colour,
the splendour of your Being, as the colourless water is flooded
with the crimson of the wine.
At the words of consecration let me be changed
changed by the miracle of your love into yourself.
In the chalice of your sacrifice, lift me to Our Father.

CARYLL HOUSELANDER

Learning to grow

Bible reading

Once I had considered Bible reading a dull chore. College courses in which we studied the Bible as literature had not changed that concept.

But after I made an act of committing my life to God, gradually for me, the Bible underwent a transformation. I wanted to read the Bible because it told me so much about the character and ways of God. I found myself eager to know how He dealt with men and women in every imaginable circumstance.

I came to understand that God means that all lives be lived in co-operation with Him. His friendship, His plans for us, His riches are awaiting us, provided we want Him in our lives... the riches of grace must be claimed. *Ye have not, because ye ask not—* the Apostle James cried.

CATHERINE MARSHALL

Appreciating the sparrows

Suddenly I began to know the water birds. They had usually been too far away and too much confused by glare for positive identification without the help of binoculars. Now with the glasses I found grebes, all sorts of ducks, and many kinds of sandpipers frequenting our bay and grassy shores... The glasses were of Japanese make, excellent both in field of vision and clarity, and from then on it was not uncommon for the trip to the post office to take an hour instead of fifteen minutes, while the neighbours saw the 'parson' peering into the woods with her binoculars. I thought, occasionally, that if I were as concerned with finding a new convert as I was in spotting a new bird, the Kingdom of God would prosper faster. Yet reverence for the ways of God with little birds certainly made me more aware of His care for His human children. Perhaps if one is to know what Jesus meant when he said, 'Ye are of more value than many sparrows,' he has to learn to really value and appreciate the sparrows first. Anyhow, that's my alibi!

MARGARET K. HENRICHSEN

Lessons for living

I was told of a series of lectures… These lectures opened up a new world of adventure, a spiritual world—an introduction to the mystery and dynamic force of prayer. Unlike other turns in the road of life, this experience was of slow growth—full of retreat, of backsliding, to use an old evangelical word. I do not think it possible to exaggerate the importance of the discoveries I made about life, and the relation of the self to the unseen world of the Spirit, and yet I find it hard to speak about; these are matters that cannot be taken on trust, they must be individually experienced and have no validity otherwise. In my case, a course of reading brought to me a sense of the *quality* of service given to the world by people like the Lady Julian of Norwich, Catherine of Siena, the Quaker Saints, Josephine Butler, and that great host of dedicated lives. My everyday trade union work took on a deeper significance. The doing of ordinary everyday things became lit up with that inner light of the Spirit which gave one strength and effectiveness; strength to meet defeat with a smile; to face success with a sense of responsibility; to be willing to do one's best without thought of reward; to bear misrepresentation without giving way to futile bitterness. Saint Theresa declared that: 'There are only two duties required of us—the love of God and the love of our neighbour, and the surest sign of discovering whether we observe these duties is the love of our neighbour': and a great scholar has asserted that this love of God is not an emotion, although that may be experienced, it is a *principle of action*—it reinforces effort, it demands that we *do* something, not merely talk or feel sympathetic, we've got to use the new strength or it will break us.

That is the vital difference between those who drift with the stream, as I did at first, and those who, like the great souls down the ages, inspire, revive, and strengthen the corporate life of their generation. Most of them are treated by their contemporaries as dangerous—and they are to systems out-worn and hampering.

Another lesson I learned was that the intensity of prayer is not measured by time, but by the reality and depth of one's awareness of unity with God. I learned to look on prayer not as a means of influencing the Creator in my favour, but as an awareness of the presence of God—everywhere.

I also learned a few helpful ideas about sin. Broadly speaking, I learned to recognize sin as the refusal to live up to the enlightenment we possess. To know the right order of values and deliberately to choose the lower ones. To know that, however much these values may differ with different people at different stages of spiritual growth, for one's self there must be no compromise with that which one *knows* to be the lower value.

I learned, too, that to condemn others is a grave mistake, since hatred, and even the wrong kind of criticism, is an evil which recoils upon its author and poisons every human relationship. It has enabled me to get some little glimpse of the meaning behind that great truth—that all the living are as one in the Great Life of the Universe. It gives meaning to life, and a happiness which nothing else can give and no one but ourselves can take away. It is a road to be travelled with a shout of joy— a most exciting road!

MARGARET BONDFIELD

Learning faith, hope and love

When we first begin to follow Christ's way of life, our knowledge of it is very embryonic and elementary, and yet we are inclined to think that we have the whole secret. We regard it as unnecessary to train ourselves in those sensitizing obediences which are the condition of receiving the heavenly grace that alone brings the flower and the fruit. Faith, hope and love have to be learned with infinite patience through a long time. They are the demands of a Creator who knew what He would have us be. We cannot pursue them feebly and attain in the Christian life. They are supreme ends which we cannot allow to be crowded out of our lives by a host of lesser purposes.

FLORENCE ALLSHORN

The disciplines of life

What have I learned in these last six years? That Spirit-motivated *disciplines* facilitate the Christian walk. Oh, I'm not discounting all the warm feelings along the road, when I've sung Jesus-songs and held hands and the rest. But our sensuous age forgets that feelings come and feelings leave you, but the disciplines of life are what get you to where you want to go.

ANNE ORTLUND

Keep the path clear

God is always pressing towards us with love, but He needs the open path of our basic commitment in order to care for us as He longs to do. We decide whether or not we will clear the path or keep it cluttered with doubts.

EUGENIA PRICE

A gift of faith

A brilliant light of hope and peace filled my soul. At once, I knew not how, the terror fled away... A deep conviction came to me that my life was accepted by God... This unusual experience at the outset of my medical career has had a lasting and marked effect on my whole life. To me it was a revealed experience of Truth, a direct vision of the great reality of spiritual existence, as irresistible as it is incommunicable. I shall be grateful to the last day of my life for this great gift of faith.

ELIZABETH BLACKWELL

The hardest lesson

True resignation is the hardest lesson in the whole school of Christ. It is the oftenest taught and the latest learnt... The submission of yesterday does not exonerate us from the resignation of today.

HANNAH MORE

Facing the facts

All sinners together

Remember, my dear, I give advice that is rather more human and sympathetic than orthodox... the root reason is that I *dare* not give unctuous and rigid counsel to anyone, because I am so profoundly and always conscious of being a sinner myself, not in imagination but in reality and with a ghastly accumulation of irrefutable proof. Consequently I *dare* not say to people, 'You must do this or that because it would be right,' knowing full well that if I were in their shoes I would do something very much *more* wrong than they should.

CARYLL HOUSELANDER

Down-to-earth holiness

The Holy Spirit never inspires anything contrary to the love of God. I pray God to grant you perseverance. What you need is patience, for in patience you shall preserve your soul.

JULIAN OF NORWICH (TO MARGERY KEMP)

If Jesus is for us...

Yes, it is true, the Church is full of all sorts of people, sinners true enough, like me, I know that. I know the promises I make and fail miserably to keep, my bad temper, my impatience. I know well enough, and I have enough people who draw my attention to them frequently—which doesn't always help my temper either! Being a minister in a small church in a small town means a rather goldfish-like existence; nothing escapes attention, particularly what I am doing, saying or looking like! And that goes for all those who dare to call themselves the friends of Jesus. The wonderful thing is, though, Jesus offers his friendship and his love to sustain us day by day. It doesn't matter what others think about us, whether they consider we are beyond the pale or not, whether they can point their fingers at our shortcomings and failures. What matters is that Jesus loves us, and is not ashamed to be called our friend. He understands us, knows our weaknesses, and will help us.

MARGARET CUNDIFF

Christ in the sinner

I saw too the reverence that everyone must have for a sinner; instead of condoning his sin, which is in reality his utmost sorrow, one must comfort Christ who is suffering in him. And this reverence must be paid even to those sinners whose souls seem to be dead, because it is Christ, who is the life of the soul, who is dead in them; they are His tombs, and Christ in the tomb is potentially the risen Christ. For the same reason, no one of us who has fallen into mortal sin himself must ever lose hope.

CARYLL HOUSELANDER

Chance after chance

As I look at my life I see areas of hardness, of shallow 'promises, promises' which never get anywhere, areas of preoccupation with my own life, with what I want to do, what I want to be. I allow these things to put a stranglehold on my effective ministry, but it's often not until I feel the life being squeezed from me that I come to my senses. It is often a very painful process, and could have been avoided if I had taken more care.

The joy is, though, that the sower does not sow once, but over and over again, year in year out. He never gives up, because he is confident of a harvest. In the book of Isaiah there is a promise which I hold on to, and it is this: 'My word is like the snow and the rain that come down from the sky to water the earth... So also will be the word that I speak—it will not fail to do what I plan for it; it will do everything I send it to do' (Isaiah 55:10–11).

God does not give up on me or you; we get chance after chance. But how sad that we waste those chances so often, when we could have been beautiful and useful if only we had listened and received what he had for us.

MARGARET CUNDIFF

Run and ask forgiveness

'Lie down and be discouraged' is always our temptation. Our feeling is that it is presumptuous, and even almost impertinent, to go at once to the Lord, after having sinned against Him. It seems as if we ought to suffer the consequences of our sin first for a little while, and endure the accusings of our conscience; and we can hardly believe that the Lord *can* be willing at once to receive us back into loving fellowship with Himself.

A little girl once expressed this feeling to me, with a child's outspoken candour. She had asked whether the Lord Jesus always forgives us for our sins as soon as we asked Him, and I had said, 'Yes, of course He does.' '*Just* as soon?' she repeated doubtingly. 'Yes,' I replied, 'the very minute we ask, He forgives us.' 'Well,' she said deliberately, 'I cannot believe that. I should think He would make us feel sorry for two or three days first. And then I should think He would make us ask Him a great many times, and in a very pretty way too, not just in common talk. And I believe that *is* the way He does, and you need not try to make me think He forgives me right at once, no matter what the Bible says.' She only *said* what most Christians *think*, and what is worse, what most Christians act on, making their discouragement and their very remorse separate them infinitely further off from God than their very sin would have done. Yet it is so totally contrary to the way we like our children to act towards us, that I wonder how we ever could have conceived such an idea of God. How a mother grieves when a naughty child goes off alone in despairing remorse, and doubts her willingness to forgive; and how, on the other hand, her whole heart goes out in welcoming love to the repentant little one who runs to her at once and begs forgiveness! Surely our God felt this yearning love when He said to us, 'Return, ye backsliding children, and I will heal your backslidings.'

The fact is, that the same moment which brings the consciousness of sin ought to bring also the confession and the consciousness of forgiveness.

HANNAH WHITALL SMITH

The real redemption of sin

The world of nature gives us an inner satisfaction when we see how all the waste and surplus, the abortive beginnings and the mistakes, are used as the basis of new life… We know, too, that we can never be satisfied unless human evil, the evil will, SIN, is dealt with in a similar way. Not just conquered and slain like a dragon, but so purged, so transformed that it is able to be used once again as material for living. That is what Redemption must accomplish; and it always must involve sacrificing and dying.

MARY F. SMITH

Give me your grace

Lord, You know me. I am so set in my ways at times.
I am stubborn, self-centred and so sure I know it all.
I must make you angry at times. Yet you love me,
you are sorry for me, you want to give me so much.
Give me the grace to admit when I am wrong, to turn from
my self and accept your love, your way, your will,
today and always.

MARGARET CUNDIFF

Love without strings

For many people, especially those alone and isolated, the closest friend they have is not a human being but an animal and animals too can become the mediators of God's grace. It did not matter to me what my own dog did—ignore me, bite me, prefer the company of someone else, refuse to do what he was told. I loved him far too much to be angry with him. One day, when we were watching television together, I realized that just as there were no strings attached to my love for George so there are no strings to God's love for us. This had a profound effect upon me—it healed my constant disabling guilt and fear at being a 'sinner' and deserving God's wrath and set me free to become less preoccupied with myself and more concerned with others.

ELIZABETH STUART

Trying too hard

My carefully book-learned principles of child care collapsed when I saw such successful results coming out of comparative neglect. In mothering, as in Christianity, we mess things up by striving too earnestly, obeying too literally, working too scrupulously: we cannot replace grace by effort.

MARGARET HEBBLETHWAITE

Only afterwards

Through the resurrection of Jesus, God reveals that he is the one who brings life from death and wholeness from brokenness. The important fact so often overlooked in this revelation is that wholeness, healing and salvation only come after and through the human experience of alienation, suffering and death. One cannot be completely healed until one has been utterly broken.

ELIZABETH STUART

Witness through weakness

If we look at various passages in scripture we see that Jesus makes some of his strongest points through those who would have been regarded as the weaker members in the society of the day—the healing of the blind man, the man who was sick of the palsy, the man with the withered hand and the healing of Legion for example. All these people would have been seen as social outcasts, the non-achievers, and yet Jesus shows us what can be achieved by faith. If God gave me such a clear message, then it suggested that, if He wanted me to witness through my weakness, the obstacles confronting me would be overcome.

LIN BERWICK

God in our failure

If you have ever been sickened by the crumbling of some enterprise into which you had put all your best effort and the love of your heart, you are caught up in the fellowship of Christ's death and resurrection, whether or not you thought of your experience in that way. God has dealt with our failure by himself becoming a failure in Jesus Christ and so healing it from the inside. That is why we can meet him in our failure; it is a sure place for finding him, since he has claimed it. So central is failure to the Easter mystery that a person who has never grappled with it could scarcely claim to be Christ's friend and follower.

MARIA BOULDING

PART TWO

Real lives, real pain

Women of Spirit live in the real world. Tragedy doesn't pass them by or bounce off some supernatural protective shield.

They're in there—in the cancer ward, at their husband's or child's graveside, in the mental hospital, in prison, flat on their back with a slipped disc—suffering just like anyone else, asking the hard questions, and drawing on their faith for the answers and the strength to get through.

Not all their ideas or methods may appeal to you. These women are as different as you and I. But the pattern is still clear—wherever we lean on God, He'll be right there for us.

No insurance policy—only grace

Being human

'If you are going to live you are going to love and if you are going to love you are going to be hurt and broken.' To be human is to be broken.

ANONYMOUS, QUOTED BY ELIZABETH STUART

The grace to endure

We reviewed our theological position, which we had frequently discussed, namely, that 'the rain falls on the just and on the unjust.' We do not expect God's special intervention for us. We live now as we always have—by the natural law of cause and effect. It is a part of the human condition. If you are stricken with a fatal disease, you will die. It's that simple—and that terrible. Faith in God provides the grace to endure.

JOANN KELLEY SMITH

Failures expected

Eventually my health visitor referred us to a child guidance officer. When I went to the child clinic the sight of all those other little terrors toddling about the floor made me feel so ill that I burst into tears, and when this happened for the second time running the health visitor decided I needed help.

In due course Blossom arrived at our house... As to her advice, it was meant to be non-directive, while in fact, it had a clear moral undertone of a sort I did not like. 'You and your husband are both very religious, I gather,' she said, 'How does that affect your feelings about Dominic?' 'It helps', I said. Blossom looked surprised and immediately changed the subject. I had given the wrong answer—I was meant to say it instilled guilt feelings. But I had probably found more solace than anywhere else in the Christian understanding that we all fail, that my failures in the field where I most wanted to succeed were not only forgivable but to be expected.

MARGARET HEBBLETHWAITE

Give me courage

Lord Jesus,
When you rode into Jerusalem on Palm Sunday,
  you knew it was the road to the cross,
    yet you still took that road.
Give me the courage to take the road I should today,
  whatever it may mean, wherever it may lead.
May I travel trustfully and obediently through this day,
  content to leave tomorrow in your safe hands,
    and tonight rest in your peace.

MARGARET CUNDIFF

Not an insurance policy

One lesson I have learned in all this is that Christians cannot expect to have charmed lives. One of my initial reactions to John's death was identical to that of the majority of people who face tragedy—'Why should this happen to me?' Now I see the answer to that question is: 'Why not?' Being a Christian is not a sort of insurance policy. We must take the knocks as well and as much as anybody else. Christian happiness cannot be rooted in other people, in health or worldly fortunes. It must rest in the assurance that we have a Heavenly Father who will see that all things work together for good.

Finally, if I was to say what, on looking back, were the great healing factors in my distress I would have to say there was something intangible and something very tangible indeed. The intangible was a sense felt even in my times of blackest despair that I was not alone. Jesus never left me for one second. He was always there in the darkness, almost as real as a physical presence. Always, there was the knowledge that He had endured an even greater darkness for our sakes, and He understood and had experienced death in a way we never shall, because He has conquered death. In my suffering I caught a tiny glimpse of part of the cost of our salvation.

The tangible factor was simply people. It was the practical things that people did which made so much difference: coming to visit me even when they couldn't find words to say; writing letters especially sharing their own experiences of bereavement; offering me a job when I needed one, listening to my woes, and above all, treating me as a normal human being when I felt anything but!...

My greatest comfort in the blackest days was the very presence and understanding of Christ Himself, and the tremendous sense of being part of the Body of Christ, with a great awareness of the love and prayers of the dedicated Christians who stood by me. Their prayers upheld and carried me along where alone I would have fallen...

BARBARA PILLER

Bad times—and good

Jesus, I praise you because I have known sickness and pain,
I praise you because I have known poverty,
failure and contempt,
I praise you because I have been falsely accused
and misjudged,
I praise you because I have suffered the parting of death,
I praise you because I have lived in sordid surroundings, and
I praise you for your goodness in bringing me to a happy
home and giving the Faith to my friend.
Grant that I may always sip from the Chalice I am unworthy
to drink from, and support me every moment with the
strong enfolding arm of your Love.

CARYLL HOUSELANDER

Unshakeable foundation

Though I know I would rather go through the gall bladder operation again than have another breakdown, I can see that my experience of mental illness was not in vain. Naturally, for a start I have learned to treat the whole subject of mental health with a new respect. My wild ideas about 'loony bins' and the mentally sick have been drastically revised, and it has been a great help to talk things through with a Christian friend who is a psychiatrist. Not only can I understand a little better the reasons for certain methods of treatment but I also feel I understand my illness and its causes a little better.

This raises the question of Christians and psychiatry. I have met several people who, though not prepared to say that a Christian should not have a breakdown, still feel a Christian should not be treated by a non-Christian psychiatrist. As there is a shortage of Christians in psychiatry this creates obvious problems! I can only speak from my own experience. I was under two psychiatrists, neither of whom made any claims to be a Christian. One was clearly in disagreement with my religious convictions, the other took a more neutral position. Nevertheless I regained my health and my faith was restored the stronger for the whole experience.

In the end I think the trouble lies with the patient, not within the treatment. I don't believe a non-Christian psychiatrist is going to set out to 'destroy a patient's faith'. It is more likely that the breakdown or illness will do that anyway. No, the testing of my breakdown was the testing of the strength of God's grip on me and my hold on Him. If my faith had been more feeble or misplaced in a shallow, frothy Christianity instead of the sure Word of God I think my recovery would have made a different story, whether I had a Christian psychiatrist or not.

Then I was on 'drugs' for over a year: tranquillizers and sleeping tablets by the bottle. Again I have heard some

Christians say a Christian should not need to take drugs. Was I failing God then? Only if I also believe that Christians should never have breakdowns and that I cannot accept. A breakdown is an illness with causes and symptoms like any other illness. If the doctor prescribes aspirin for influenza and I take those, then why should I not take tranquillizers and sleeping tablets to relieve the symptoms of mental illness?

So where some would look only for the harmful effects of psychiatry and drugs I can see only blessing and fruitfulness.

The breakdown has given me a foundation deep within my spiritual experience that is unshakeable, tested as the onslaught of the illness stormed at the defences of my faith and tore away my immature, untested ideas whittling my experience of God down to its basics. I look back and claim the promise of John 10 that no one can snatch me from His hand. No experience can be worse than the agony of that breakdown. I can face the future secure in His grip.

MARY ENDERSBEE

Living as Christ's people

We wanted no groups rallying to pray for the unexpected miracle—nor did we want new cures, healers, or quack remedies to cope with or raise our hopes...

We would accept a miracle if it came as God's gift, but we would not dare plan for it... For us, the reality of living through this experience as Christ's people would have a far deeper meaning for our family than would prayers to single us out for the gift of a miracle that might never come.

JOANN KELLEY SMITH

Communion

He is still on earth in the host,
He is crucified in the Mass
And in my Communion
rises again in me.

...

Whatever I have to suffer
However hardly I die to self,
He will rise in me.

However numbed I have been
By even the greatest sorrow,
The cruellest disappointment,
He will rise again in me.

CARYLL HOUSELANDER

God is there for us

Words of strength

He did not say 'You shall not be tempest-tossed, you shall not be work-weary, you shall not be discomforted.' But he said, 'You shall not be overcome.'

JULIAN OF NORWICH

He meets me

In searching for God's purpose—the reasons behind events—I saw that whenever I had come to Jesus stripped of pretensions, with a needy spirit, ready to listen to Him and to receive what He had for me, He had met me at my point of need. *He can make the difference in every human situation.*

The word 'impossible' melts away with Him. He knows no defeat; can turn every failure and frustration into unexpected victory. He can reverse a doctor's grim prognosis. With Him a seemingly dark and desolate future becomes a joyous new life.

I know all this to be true because I have lived it. I have met God at moments when the straight road turns... and He has picked me up, wiped away my tears, and set me back on the path of life.

CATHERINE MARSHALL

Faith reaffirmed

When I was hospitalized for my mastectomy, I thought, this could be it, and only God can help me. Through prayer, I let go and turned it over. This was before I knew I was alcoholic, before I had ever heard these phrases. Tension dissolved, my mind and my whole body relaxed, it was as though a huge weight had been lifted from me, as though a light had gone on. God was in my life. He would take care of me, and I was going to be all right. That day, my faith in God was reaffirmed in such a strong way that it has never really faltered since.

BETTY FORD

Not broken

During the war, I was simply terrified by air raids, and it was my lot to be in every one that happened in London... I tried to build up my courage by reason and prayer, etc., etc. Then one day I realized quite suddenly: as long as I try not to be afraid I shall be worse, and I shall show it one day and break; what God is asking of me, to do for suffering humanity, is to *be* afraid, to accept it and put up with it... Instead of kidding myself and trying to minimize the danger or to find some distraction from it, I said to myself: 'For as long as this raid lasts—an hour—or eight hours—you are going to be terrified... so you must carry on and *be* terrified, that's all.'—and at once the *strain* ceased. Oh yes, I was terrified:... But all that time I felt that God had put His hand right down through all the well upon well of darkness and horror between Him and me and was holding the central point of my soul; and I knew that *however* afraid I was then, it would not, even could not, break me... It's only when we try *not* to experience our special suffering that it can really break us.

CARYLL HOUSELANDER

Real peace

Real peace does not mean we suddenly are transported to a problem-free realm where nothing bad ever happens. Real peace means we can survive the chaos and confusion around us without becoming chaotic or confused.

There is no such thing as 'easy peace'... If you recite the 23rd Psalm every night before you go to sleep and really think about it, you will be soothed temporarily. But you will only be really strengthened inwardly, you will only be given real, tough, durable, inner *peace*, if you come to realize and recognize the firm grip of the hand of the One who *is* already your Shepherd!

EUGENIA PRICE

A mother's fears

As mothers we need to be able to turn to God with our fears. Every time the children are late or lost or running a temperature of 104° we need to be able to put our trust in someone more powerful than ourselves, and say 'Please God, you love them too. Please let it be all right.' If we are able to trust in God's love it is much easier to survive these cliff-hanging worries...

MARGARET HEBBLETHWAITE

A mother's last words to her daughter

I am very, very glad when I think of you, because your whole life is given to your Saviour and I know that one day He will say to you, 'Enter into the joy of thy Lord'.

He does satisfy the heart of His loving, trusting child. You have found Him true, I know, just as I have, and tens of thousands have. No one who gave herself wholly to Him was ever disappointed at the end. No, not one.

And all the time He is with you, my child. He says to you, 'Daughter, thou art ever with Me and all that I have is thine.' He notices everything, remembers everything, gives everything His dear child needs for life and service. She is ever with Him, never, never far away from His loving heart.

If this note is ever in your hands it will be because I am out of sight, with the Lord. But I shall not be forgetting you. I do not forget you now although I see you so seldom. I shall be thinking of you, loving you, praying for you, rejoicing as I see you run your race.

God bless you and make you a blessing.

AMY CARMICHAEL

Turn the carpet

This world which clouds thy soul with doubt
Is but a carpet inside out;
As when we view these shreds and ends,
We know not what the whole intends;
So when on earth things look but odd,
They're working out some scheme of God.

What now seems random strokes will there
In order and design appear.
Then we shall praise what here we spurn'd,
For then the carpet shall be turn'd.

HANNAH MORE

A wonderful friend

Although prison conditions were very hard, hope remained with me. I experienced no sorrow, my spirit was not depressed by fear. I was able to live through these three years with the words from St Matthew, chapter 11, verse 30 before my eyes: 'For my yoke is easy and my burden is light.' Though these words from the Bible were very familiar to me before my arrest, only now do I understand how true and correct they are. Christ's burden is indeed light to bear. I experienced this in a deep way in prison many times. During my time there I had a wonderful friend, the risen Lord Jesus Christ. I experienced in prison the same as did a Christian sister, who wrote from her cell that Christ gives His grace and presence to those in prison, so that one is able to endure what lies ahead. We're never alone or rejected, not even in prison.

AIDA SKRIPNIKOVA

Opening the door to the Spirit

'At that moment I didn't want anything except for God to take me quickly—as I was. I said, "God, I don't know who You are. I don't know anything about You. I don't even know how to pray. Just, Lord, have Your own way with me."'

Though she did not realize it, Maude Blanford had just prayed one of the most powerful of all prayers—the prayer of relinquishment. By getting her own mind and will out of the way, she had opened the door to the Holy Spirit...

Gradually, as her knowledge of Him grew, she sensed His protective love surrounding and sheltering her. Not that all pain and difficulties were over. She was still on pain-numbing drugs, still experiencing much nausea as the aftermath of the radiation.

'The will to live is terribly important,' she commented... 'It takes a lot of self-effort just to get out of bed, to eat again after your food has just come up. This is when too many people give up.'

It took time... nine months for her bad leg to be near normal, two years for all symptoms of cancer to vanish.

MAUDE BLANFORD, AS TOLD TO CATHERINE MARSHALL

Perfect peace

[T]wo days past November 18, which was hysterectomy day for me... The night before surgery, the last words I read were these: 'May all God's mercies and peace be yours from God our Father and from Jesus Christ our Lord' (Romans 1:7, TLB). I thought about all God's mercies: his loving concern for me, his tenderly watching over me more efficiently even than doctors and machines and charts. I thought about his peace: the sense of well-being he gives...

One of the disciplines of a godly woman must be the discipline of the mind. We are not free to let our emotions flip and flop all over the place. We are not free to fret and worry if we feel like it, to indulge ourselves in pouting and stewing. That doesn't mean that the blues aren't permissible; they are. Many of the Psalms are David's laying out his feelings openly before the Lord—his 'down' feelings as well as his 'up' feelings...

But *anxiety*—that's something else. Worry is disobedience. The disciplined mind makes no room for doubting God's plans for me...

'Thou wilt keep him in perfect peace, whose mind is stayed on thee; because he trusteth in thee' (Isaiah 26:3, KJV). ... Life has no other soft pillow but that! All else is steep precipices and darkness and sudden new violence. But in you, Lord—in your will, in your presence—*all is well*.

ANNE ORTLUND

Recovery from alcoholism

At the beginning of my recovery, I read everything I could find about alcoholism and treatment... A friend put me on to a collection called *The Great Texts of the Bible*, and, searching the index for some reference to alcoholism, I found Numbers 32, verse 23—'Be sure your sin will find you out'... Well, this treatise was written in the early 1900s, when they didn't know alcoholism was a disease, and not a sin. Today we believe the sin is in not doing something about it.

I have found sobriety brings balance, and balance brings serenity. In recovery, I have sometimes lost this balance, and it usually happens when I am neglecting my spiritual program. Then all the chronic symptoms—envy, resentment, self-pity, anger—of my disease reappear. Like most alcoholics, I handle anger badly, and I try to deal with this by writing out what is making me angry, and when I put it down on paper, I realize how I'm allowing it to disrupt my life. And this realization permits me to move along. I really do believe that God never gives us more than we can handle. But I also believe He expects us to do the footwork, we can't just sit back and wait for Him to dump everything in our laps.

BETTY FORD

The everlasting arms

It was not till the morning of the operation that I suddenly thought, 'I might die this afternoon!' Until then I had been completely free of fear. At once God asked me the old question, 'If you *should* die, do you believe that I will be with you?' My answer was, of course, 'Yes!' and my fear left me. It was replaced by the thought, 'Underneath are the everlasting arms, and they never fail, or falter.' I was often to lie back on those arms during the next days, and they were always there, giving peace, security, and something that I could give to those around me and to my many visitors.

JOAN PORTER BUXTON

God brings about the issue

Have faith in God. Faith is really believing that a *good* will come to pass in spite of things that are looking clean contrary. Disbelief, indifference, boredom, fear, they will come at you like swarms of gnats. Watch, from outside yourself. Go on believing in the truth. Whether the thing that baffles you (that personal relationship) looks possible or impossible is really not your question. You have your task in it, but you will be beaten in it if you let go faith in the facts that God also has His task in it. He will bring about the issue, not you.

FLORENCE ALLSHORN

Reach out in power and love

Suffering and death are real. I only have to pick up the papers to know that. It is there, recorded in stark words and pictures.

Suffering and death are real. I know it from my own experience, and I am afraid.

In your love and power reach out to those who suffer today, to those who mourn, those who have lost hope.

Reach out to me too, Lord, and grant me your peace.

MARGARET CUNDIFF

On death and dying

Voice of experience

I think a lot of old people just aren't very sensible. They only have old friends and then they live to be ninety or something, like me, and then they start moaning because their friends have gone before, as they say.

My advice to the aged woman is find some young people. Don't go to these dreadful old folks' clubs but find some young people. Put up with their casualness because it's worth it. Why, I should like to know, are they so casual, I wonder?

I don't dread dying in my sleep, but I do dread dying any other way. Mostly for the nuisance, you know. And I don't dread being dead. My heavenly Father has looked after me from the cradle and he won't stop at the grave. Through all my life he has taken care of me. Even if I just went out like a candle, what is there to dread?

CLERGYMAN'S WIDOW

In death and eternal life

[My mother's] death was another moment of truth for me. Till then ever since I had tried to live God's way, I had felt sure that if you did this, He kept you safe and shielded you from danger, pain or tragedy. Now I learned that even if God does not send pain, neither does He always protect you from it. He goes through it with you, and, if you will let Him, uses it for others over and over again. I also found that my faith in the eternal life, in continuing unity with those we love, was not only strengthened, but that real love for them meant that you truly let them go into God's keeping and trusted them to Him. I often have the feeling that those I love are near, but I am also sure that if I demand to have that sense of their presence, I really do hold them back from the fullness of God's on-going plan for them.

JOAN PORTER BUXTON

Shadows of glory

Though death walks at my heels,
and welcome,
this is the beginning,
not the end of my story.
I walk among shadows,
O Liege Lord,
my love,
Shadows
of Your bright glory!

CARYLL HOUSELANDER

Fearing death

To fear death doesn't make me less of a Christian. It affirms my humanity.

But most of us are afraid of any new experience because we fear the unknown.

I have a better chance to adjust to a new experience if I have a few clues as to what to expect. But there are very few to guide us in death. We just say to God, 'I'm yours.'

JOANN KELLEY SMITH

No fear

I can never see why one should fear to die. When I walk into the garden here early in the morning and nearly burst with excitement at this world; and when I realize that it is only a shadow, a pale ghost of what *that* world must be like—then I can only feel a tremendous longing to know more of it, and to be in it.

FLORENCE ALLSHORN

The leap of faith

God has not deserted me in life. Neither will he in death. And I have confidence he knows the way. I'm apprehensive and often frightened, but just as I have taken the leap of faith before, I'm prepared for this one. I believe that whatever God has in store for me, as his person, it will be better than the life I've enjoyed here—great as that has been...

Out of the Second World War comes the story of a father and his daughter seeking refuge from the bombs that showered London. He found a deep crater, which he thought would offer safety and took shelter there. He called to his daughter, telling her to jump. She was afraid of the darkness below and said, 'But I can't see you.' And he replied, 'It's all right—I can see you.' So she jumped and was caught in his waiting arms. We can't see God waiting for us. But he can see us. That's the leap of faith.

JOANN KELLEY SMITH

Relinquishing loved ones

Well, it's true we are in God's hands, and, as I meant to say, and may have said to you before, the only prayer I can say now is 'Into Thy hands, Father, into Thy hands'—and it is not only my wretched body and shivering soul that I am at last committing absolutely to the hands of Infinite Love, but, and this is so much greater a surrender, all those whom I love... above all, those whom I presumed to feel dependent on my love.

CARYLL HOUSELANDER

Good out of evil

Hard times, and sweet

Let us so bind ourselves
that we will not only
adhere to You
in times of consolation,
in times of sweetness and devotion
and when life goes smoothly,
but yet more securely
in the bleak and bitter
seasons of the soul—
in the iron hard winters
of the spirit.

CARYLL HOUSELANDER

Enid's meditation

Enid fought her way to peace and we often had to battle alongside her. She found her profound dependence hard to bear and could be difficult and demanding. Such struggles towards acceptance are often prolonged as the same battle is fought over and over again and never seems to be finished. She asked sometimes angry but honest questions of the God she deeply believed in and had served during her active life, and after a long battle she gradually accepted the reality of what was happening and found the answer which she has left us, dictated during the month before she died.

'A friend and I were considering life and its purpose. I said, even with increasing paralysis and loss of speech, I believed there was a purpose for my life, but I was not sure what it was at that particular time. We agreed to pray about it for a week. I was then sure that my present purpose is simply to receive other people's prayers and kindness and to link together all those who are lovingly concerned about me, many of whom are unknown to one another. After a while my friend said: "It must be hard to be the wounded Jew when, by nature, you would rather be the Good Samaritan."

It is hard: it would be unbearable were it not for my belief that the wounded man and the Samaritan are inseparable. It was the helplessness of the one that brought out the best in the other and linked them together.

In reflecting on the parable, I am particularly interested in the fact that we are not told the wounded man recovered. I have always assumed that he did, but now it occurs to me that even if he did not recover, the story will still stand as a perfect example of true neighbourliness. You will remember the story concludes with the Samaritan asking the innkeeper to take care of the man, but he assures him of his own continuing interest and support; so, the innkeeper becomes linked.

If, as my friend suggested, I am cast in the role of the wounded man, I am not unmindful of the modern day counterparts of the Priest and Levite, but I am overwhelmed by the kindness of so many 'Samaritans'. There are those who, like you, have been praying for me for a long time and constantly reassure me of continued interest and support. There are many others who have come into my life—people I would never have met had I not been in need, who are now being asked to take care of me. I like to think that all of us have been linked together for a purpose which will prove a means of blessing to us all.'

ENID HENKE, WITH COMMENT BY CICELY SAUNDERS

Lesson in pain

As we stood waiting for our bus to take us back to our friend's home my back began to hurt. By the time we got home I hardly knew how to stand. In an hour or two I could not move my left leg and was having cramp up that side and pain such as I had never known before. In fact, it proved to be a slipped disc, but a very painful one, and I was to lie there, literally helpless, for nearly a month...

I learned one very big thing about pain. I am not by nature a person who bears pain gladly or easily. At first I just lay there and prayed for the moment when I would be given pain-killing drugs. Then one day God said very clearly to me, 'Let go and give yourself to your pain. Stop resisting it. It is a way in which to a small degree you can enter into some understanding of My pain on the Cross.' It was not easy to follow that out, but I kept on trying, and I have never forgotten that lesson. Ever since, whenever pain, whether physical or emotional, has come my way I have tried to face it in that spirit. Pain for me now is no longer an enemy to be resisted at all costs. Rather, if God allows it I can accept it as His gift, asking Him to go through it with me, and then I find that invariably He uses it in some way to help or to understand the need of someone else. Obviously, I do not always succeed, but it is something to aim at and it undercuts self-pity and resentment.

JOAN PORTER BUXTON

Real healing

What do we mean when we speak of 'healing'? For some, it will be miraculous restoration of physical health but, for me, healing can come in many different ways. Healing can be the response by one human being to another in warmth and love and friendship. It can be doing something thoughtful or kindly. Perhaps our Lord does not always want us to receive *physical* healing. Certainly, in my case, I am anything but outwardly whole, yet inwardly I feel a complete person. Knowing that I have received *inner* health and healing, having been given a strength that can only come from God, I feel that God wants me to use my weakness to project His strength to others.

I know that my disability has given me greater compassion. It has enabled me to get alongside other human beings and share their sufferings simply because I have had a degree of suffering myself and therefore I can identify with them.

LIN BERWICK

Entitled—by suffering

I thanked God for my experiences in the concentration camp. Now I could tell these people about my experience of the reality of Jesus Christ in the hell of Ravensbruck. The fact that I also had suffered aroused their interest, and I was entitled to speak, because I could understand them.

CORRIE TEN BOOM

I can tell...

In adult life the word cancer was my secret, hidden fear, the unmentionable thing, spoken only in whispers. Yet from the moment I heard the word and knew the specialist was speaking about me, I have been released from all fears, both great and small... because I'm a woman, because I write, because I go to lots of women's meetings as a speaker, I can talk about women's problems, I can tell about my four years of hopping in and out of a sick bed, major operations, radium treatment—and I can tell them how I manage to cope with the commitments and give reassuring news of the progress that is being made by research.

I have so many blessings that it is impossible to count them and I can only thank God for my sixteen wonderful years in which I have realized day by day and hour by hour the wonderful truth of God's caring power.

JOSEPHINE HILTON

Love creates love

I know what it can feel like to part from a man whom one is in love with, for I too have done so, years and years ago... I have never had any 'feeling' of his nearness or anything since he died, but I have always *known* that he is alive and that one day, I devoutly hope, we shall meet... Also, and maybe this is more important, *because* I loved that man I have loved many other people, animals and things.

CARYLL HOUSELANDER

When it goes wrong

But sometimes it does seem to go wrong, and God's love seems incomprehensible. I have two friends whose babies have died, one at ten weeks, the other at one week...

Those babies who died were real persons, as their mothers knew they were... To all eternity they will exist as human persons, and yet what kind of eternity can we imagine for them? We cannot imagine. We cannot envision how God can bring to fruition in eternity the personality lost to this world. What did they achieve in this world? Only a message of the existence of love, a love whose size can be measured by the size of the pain that it leaves behind.

MARGARET HEBBLETHWAITE

When disaster comes

When disaster first makes its unwelcome appearance into our lives, self-pity is the first, unavoidable, normal and probably right reaction. Courage flies out at the window, the world seems all of a sudden hostile and menacing, an alien place where we are no longer at home. We feel as though we are falling apart, and are deaf to everything but the shriek of our own misery. In the early stages I don't see how it is possible to fight self-pity. We only exhaust ourselves in trying to keep it at bay. But there is a time-limit, and we alone can fix it. I believe it is possible to recognize the point of no return, the moment when self-pity threatens to become malignant. And that is when we have to stand firm, for if once we allow it to get a real hold we are doomed. Self-pity is a cancer which erodes not only our courage and our will to happiness, but also our humanity and our capacity to love. It destroys us, and it destroys the friends who love us and who want to help. After all, if we come to see ourselves as the ill-used victims of outrageous fate, all our actions and thoughts will be governed by bitterness, rancour and sour envy.

In the normal rush and hullabaloo of life, we have neither time nor mind for personal stock-taking. It is only when we are brought up short, when we are afraid or bewildered or disoriented, that we turn to God with an uncomprehending, frequently agnostic, cry for help. The bubble of our self-esteem has been pricked, our complacency has gone, and we are totally vulnerable. Then and only then can grace begin to operate in us, when we begin to take stock of ourselves, and to listen to our inner voices.

Is it really paradoxical that when we are distressed we turn to the friend who knows what distress can be like? We don't know why, but there doesn't seem much point in going for sympathy, the deep-down, understanding kind, to those other friends whose paths have always been smooth. It is as though human beings lack a whole dimension and cannot come to maturity until they have faced sorrow. There is an old Arab proverb which says 'Too much sunshine makes a desert' and the human heart is very often a desert. But sorrow irrigates the desert. A few years ago a friend of mine, a poet, stricken by the death of a close friend, wrote:

Shall I complain
How swift you passed?
Could I regret the widened heart?
Could I complain of it at all?

CICELY SAUNDERS AND MARY CRAIG

Blessings outweigh

When I compare all my blessings with the things that are wrong, the blessings far outweigh the petty clashes and the other things. I don't know what I would do without the Lord. I've certainly been far happier the last ten years with Multiple Sclerosis than I ever was, healthy and strong, before I knew Him.

VALERIE HADERT

Counting blessings

In my opinion, the most glorious singing voice I have ever heard was the almost unbelievably beautiful contralto voice of Kathleen Ferrier. Miss Ferrier died of cancer when she was still a young woman. From her hospital bed she wrote to a close friend: 'Well, here I sit in bed counting my blessings!'

KATHLEEN FERRIER QUOTED BY EUGENIA PRICE

Good out of all evil

Of all the feasts of the Church, Holy Innocents is the most intolerable: of all sounds after the crying of children, the most terrible is the crying of Rachel weeping for her children, because they are not. Except when she is crying because they still are. I cannot reconcile the images of tiny deformed children with old men's eyes, in great pain... with what I am bound to believe of a loving, omnipotent Father. I will not assent to this pain as anything but a manifest evil. [However] one of the most helpful things that was ever said to me was 'The definition of *Almighty* means that there is no evil out of which good cannot be brought.' This I have found, extremely painfully, to be true.

MARGARET SPUFFORD

How great is God's love

It was on a recent Good Friday that many of our congregation became caught up in a tragedy enacted right on the threshold of the church. They had gathered on the steps to sing some of the great Passion hymns before setting off in a procession of witness to carry the cross through the streets of the city. A young man, who worked in a cafe opposite, joined them to sing with them. As they reached the last hymn, he left to go back to the cafe, where a racial brawl had broken out. In the affray he was stabbed by two white teenagers. He returned to the church steps and fell dying at the feet of the people still singing a Passion hymn. They tended for him as well as they could but were unable to save his life. He died in the ambulance on the way to the hospital.

It was many months later that a woman came to the church and introduced herself as the mother of the murdered man. She had come down from her home in Manchester to visit the place where her son had died. Then she said words that none of us who heard her will ever forget.

'I want you to know,' she said, 'that I have learned through this tragedy how great is God's love. There is no one a mother can love more than her son and no loss can be greater than to see him die. But that is what God suffered for us. He saw His Son die, but He never stopped loving us. We must allow such love to fill our hearts too, not to condemn, but to save those who sin against us.'

PAULINE WEBB

God cries too

On those terrible children's wards, I could neither have worshipped nor respected any God who had not himself cried, 'My God, my God, why hast thou forsaken me?' Because it was so, because the creator loved his creation enough to become helpless with it and suffer in it, totally overwhelmed by the pain of it, I found there was still hope. But without the Garden of Gethsemane, without the torture and the gibbet, there would be no hope for any of us, overwhelmed in the present by pain.

MARGARET SPUFFORD

God grieves most of all

Of course I heard people ask how God could let such a thing happen. I heard people say they could no longer believe. But I didn't hear these things from the people of Aberfan. I heard them from the visitors, the sightseers, the newspaper reporters.

In Aberfan I heard that God grieved most of all. In Aberfan I saw them fill the churches. I saw them lean on their faith and find it strong enough. In Aberfan I found more comfort than I gave.

HETTIE TAYLOR

Share the stories

At a women's retreat in Canada, we found that it took only a few personal stories to open the floodgates of anguish and pain. Almost everyone in the room was ready to share her struggles of faith in the face of broken marriages, broken health, broken families, broken lives. There is a deep longing to redeem the scars and amputations. Offering them as a gift to others who walk the same path is a beginning... It is precisely where we have suffered and known pain that we can be instruments of life and hope to others.

GWEN CASHMORE AND JOAN PULS OSF

The people we need

I am so much a sinner that I understand well how the slightest discouragement from outside oneself, added to the chronic close-on-despair inside, can crush one altogether... One doesn't want a preacher, or even a shining example, but someone who will share the burden, even if they know they can't carry their own.

CARYLL HOUSELANDER

Affirm me

I need to know that God has not abandoned me, but accepts me with all my human weakness, my questions, my fears, my doubts, my ambivalence, and my contradictions.

I need the affirmation of my humanity that Rita gave me when she entered my hospital room and through my tears assured me, 'Don't be afraid—don't feel bad about crying—our Lord didn't want to die and he cried the night through. Even on the cross he felt the loneliness and the separation—just try to be a person—don't try to be an angel.'

JOANN KELLEY SMITH

Don't give up on me

Lord,
I so soon get thrown by circumstances.
I panic over little things,
faith goes out the window.
Be patient with me.
Remind me of all the way you have brought me,
provided for me.
Feed me with your living word
that I may grow in understanding,
in trust and love.
Don't give up on me, will you?
—But I know you won't,
because you promised you wouldn't,
and you always keep your promises.

MARGARET CUNDIFF

A happy Christ

What you have helped me to see is a very happy Christ. I can't get away from that. He's not saying, 'Be like this and you'll be good.' He's saying, 'Be like this and you'll be happy, and it's the only way of happiness.' It's not how other people affect you, it's how you affect other people that matters all the time. Give and give and give happiness, and you'll get it all the time. That's the way God has made things work, and this stupid me, wanting to get away from the pain of this place, sees now and then that *that* wouldn't make me happy. It's accepting it that makes me happy, and I have been very happy lately, since I have seen the happy Christ.

FLORENCE ALLSHORN

PART THREE

The real world

Women of Spirit are women of today—juggling busy lives, keeping homes together and seeing elderly parents and rebellious teenagers and grubby toddlers are fed and cared for. And yet they are not hermetically sealed off from the 'big issues'. In this section you'll find material from women imprisoned for living out their faith (in England as well as in Russia!)—and some clarion calls to a new vision for the (so-far) less spirited of us!

The call to action

Spend it wisely

Time is like loose change... It is given to us here below to buy
the real things of eternity... Let us use it!

JULIE BILLIART

Start where we are

In the present world of turmoil, what can *we*?

I think constantly of a saying of Luther's which, roughly
translated, runs: 'Even if the world came to an end to-morrow,
we will still, in spite of that, plant our little apple tree to-day!'

We can all start with our own hearts, our own homes,
making, if we can, a little pool of peace where others may find
refreshment. We can pray, regularly and hopefully. We can keep
our tempers, do the small household chores cheerfully, help our
neighbours, stop grumbling! Very, very insignificant things in
the face of world problems: but as the old saying goes, we can
put a drop of oil on the troubled waters; and each of us may
serve God's purpose as far as we may.

ELIZABETH FOX HOWARD

Real Christian work

In nothing has the Church so lost her hold on reality as in her failure to understand and respect the secular vocation. She has allowed work and religion to become separate departments, and is astonished to find that, as a result, the secular work of the world is turned to purely selfish and destructive ends, and the greater part of the world's intelligent workers have become irreligious, or at least, uninterested in religion. But is it astonishing? How can any one remain interested in a religion which seems to have no concern with nine-tenths of life? The Church's approach to an intelligent carpenter is usually confined to exhorting him not to be drunk and disorderly in his leisure hours, and to come to church on Sunday. What the Church *should* be telling him is that he should make good tables. Church by all means, and decent forms of amusement, certainly—but what use is all that if in the very centre of his life and occupation he is insulting God with bad carpentry? No crooked tablelegs or ill-fitting drawers ever, I dare swear, came out of the carpenter's shop at Nazareth. Nor, if they did, could anyone believe that they were made by the same hand that made heaven and earth...

Let the Church remember this: that every maker and worker is called to serve God *in* his profession or trade—not outside it... The official Church wastes time and energy, and, moreover, commits sacrilege, in demanding that secular workers should neglect their proper vocation in order to do Christian work—by which she means ecclesiastical work. The only Christian work is good work well done. Let the Church see to it that the workers are Christian people and do their work well, as to God: then all work will be Christian work, whether it is Church embroidery or sewage-farming.

DOROTHY L. SAYERS

Open

I stand.
I open myself to God.
I kneel.
I listen.
I step into God's presence.
I float in the encompassing ocean of God's love
like a sieve in the sea.
I breathe in and out:
breathing in the mercy of God,
breathing out the pain of my sadness.

I am still
at rest with God,
who is deep within me
and all around me.

Out of that deep centre
I weave a prayer
of God's presence,
affirming that God is,
that God is with the poor,
that God is with the outcast,
that God is with me.

I call upon God's Spirit.
She rests like a butterfly
shimmering on a branch.
She confronts the hurt,
which lies curled
at the heart of society.

She leads me out,
from active prayer,
into prayerful action.

KATE McILHAGGA

Drop by drop

It may be a drop in the ocean, but the ocean is made up of drops.

MOTHER TERESA

Today

You see, *God's* Will for you is to serve Him, in His way, as He chooses *now*. It is only a want of humility to think of extreme vocations, like being a nun or a nurse, while you try to by-pass your present obvious vocation... *Today* you have to use what you have today, and do not look beyond it.

CARYLL HOUSELANDER

Individuals wanted

Musicians, painters and well-known writers live on in the lives of millions of future generations who enjoy the gifts they have created. The valuable legacy they leave to the world is not of riches but in how they used their great artistic gifts. Yet all of us have been endowed with some gift which we can use to benefit humanity. I have always been surprised by the number of well-meaning people with a genuine desire to help who have looked at the enormity facing humanity and said, 'The problem is too big—there is nothing I, as an individual, can do to help.' The truth is that there are few problems confronting humanity that are incapable of solution if only a sufficient number of human beings apply their hearts and energies.

SUE RYDER

Turning the world upside down

Whoever started the rumour that Christianity is not a political faith got the wrong end of the stick. It is not only political, it is revolutionary, for it seeks to turn the world upside down and ensure that those who are now last—the poor, the sick, homeless and oppressed—will be first. A Christian will not be other-worldly, he or she will look for God in the challenge that God is presenting us with in this world.

ELIZABETH STUART

The imprint of Jesus

God must take first place in my life. That is clear in the commandments given by God and confirmed by the words of Jesus, and I am required to show that in my life by what I do, what I say, how I think, my attitude to other people, every aspect of life. It must show as clearly in my life as the imprint of a coin. Living in this country at the present time I can carry my 'dual nationality' fairly easily, and I am thankful for that; but at the same time we all have to recognize that it is not so for many people in the world today. Many pay the price of their Christian discipleship through hardship, rejection, torture and imprisonment, and many already have paid with their lives.

As I look out from my comfortable position to what has happened and is happening I am challenged afresh to look at the image of my life. What do others see as I stand beside them at the supermarket checkout, in the bus queue, as we exchange greetings in the street. What about the conversations I have, the way I use my money and time, my response to people and situations in my own community? Have I dulled the image of Jesus Christ? Overlaid it with grime and muck, allowed it to be tarnished?

MARGARET CUNDIFF

Thy Kingdom come

The life of the planet, and especially its human life, is a life in which something has gone wrong, and badly wrong. Every time that we see an unhappy face, an unhealthy body, hear a bitter or despairing word, we are reminded of that. The occasional flashes of pure beauty, pure goodness, pure love which show us what God wants and what He is, only throw into more vivid relief the horror of cruelty, greed, oppression, hatred, ugliness; and also the mere muddle and stupidity which frustrate and bring suffering into life. Unless we put on blinkers, we can hardly avoid seeing all this; and unless we are warmly wrapped up in our own cosy ideas, and absorbed in our own interests, we surely cannot help feeling the sense of obligation, the shame of acquiescence, the call to do something about it. To say day by day 'Thy Kingdom come'—if these tremendous words really stand for a conviction and desire—does not mean 'I quite hope that some day the Kingdom of God will be established, and peace and goodwill prevail. But at present I don't see how it is to be managed or what I can do about it.' On the contrary, it means, or should mean, 'Here am I! Send me!'—active, costly collaboration with the Spirit in whom we believe.

EVELYN UNDERHILL

Real power

Spiritual power is the power to influence others through one's own being—by example, by kindness, by wisdom, by love, and above all through prayer. Institutional power has to do with ambition and control, spiritual power has much to do with surrendering control.

BISHOP PENNY JAMIESON

How we love one another

In our day obedience to the second commandment has found, perhaps, its chief expression in humanitarian movements—in the desire to serve rather than love and understand. We have become excellent social servants, Christian organizers, doctors, nurses, teachers, but we have lost the essential spring of 'fellowship one with another'. People outside Christianity look at our little Christian groups, our parish churches, our Christian schools, colleges, societies, and fail to see them shining out like light in dark places. Christian committees, diocesan councils, missionary bodies, all these should be centres of light, of the Spirit—and so often they are not. Instead of 'How these Christians love one another' we hear 'I never go near church societies or parish organizations, there is so much gossip and rivalry.' The criticism would not matter if it were not so often the truth.

FLÓRENCE ALLSHORN

Down with sectarianism!

My very soul is sick of religious controversy. How I hate the little narrowing names of Arminian and Calvinist! Christianity is a broad basis. *Bible* Christianity is what I love; that does not insist on opinions indifferent in themselves;—a Christianity practical and pure, which teaches holiness, humility, repentance and faith in Christ; and which after summing up all the evangelical graces, declares that the greatest of these is charity.

HANNAH MORE

Only one course

The Church's struggle is to stand in the way of truth and follow the Lord straightforwardly, regardless of everything else. When the Church is fighting I can't remain uninvolved. One can be a militant atheist or a non-militant atheist, one can be simply a non-believer, indifferent towards both faith and atheism, but for the Christian there is only one course. The Christian can't be anything but militant. Once you know the truth, this means following it, upholding it and if necessary suffering for it. I can't be different. I can't act differently.

AIDA SKRIPNIKOVA

Ships in the night

The world is faced with bad news, and yet there is a great Christian Church which is reputed to be the custodian of good news; there is the Church's awakened evangelistic concern, and the world's bewildered groping for the light, and yet they seem to pass each other in the dark.

FLORENCE ALLSHORN

Will He find faith on earth?

Who among us has the courage to ask in our assemblies and our meeting rooms the hard question: when the Son of Man comes, will He find any faith on the earth (Luke 18:8)? For are not the implications meant for us, who plan programmes to address poverty and injustice, and regularly claim our high salaries and pursue our comfortable life-styles? For us, who preach sacrifice and generosity to our parishioners, and sport our latest-model Oldsmobiles and expensive golf clubs? For us, who profess solidarity with the poor and continue to build retirement homes and travel in style and dress like our secular counterparts? For us, who read the scriptures, while we shun the Samaritans of our day, live in discord, compete for positions, and shirk confrontation with those who perpetrate injustice? The word of the Lord to us is a call to repentance, to open our lives to conversion, and to allow the scriptures to judge and rebuke us.

JOAN PULS OSF

Do not ask...

Do not ask 'what can I do?' but 'what can He not do?'

CORRIE TEN BOOM

The servant

Once, some time ago, [God] brought to my mind the phrase, 'Jesus is among you as him that serveth.' He was teaching me to be a servant, and he gave me all sorts of boring servant things to do for a few particularly bossy people, in trying circumstances. One day I got utterly fed up. 'Lord,' I said, 'I just *hate* being a servant. I much prefer it when somebody else waits on me than when I wait on somebody else. I do it because you say so, and because you were a servant, and you want your disciples to be servants. But why? What's so special about being a servant? Couldn't you have invented something more fun for your disciples to be?'

Then he answered, something like this: 'If I came to you as a King of kings and Lord of lords, you'd be frightened. And if I came to you as one in authority, many people have hangups about those in authority, and would refuse to listen. And if I came to you as your equal, many people have rivalry situations with their equals, and would refuse to listen. But nobody is threatened by a servant. A servant is someone you order about. You can send him out of the room if you like, you needn't listen to him. He does jobs for you. I am your servant because I love you and out of my love for you I make myself available as your servant, so as not to frighten you off and so that people may be won to my love. That is why I want my disciples to be servants.'

SYLVIA MARY ALISON

A plan for charity: 18th century style

Young ladies should be accustomed to set apart a fixed part of their time, as sacred to the poor, whether in relieving, instructing, or working for them; and the performance of this duty must not be left to the event of contingent circumstances, or the operation of accidental impressions; but it must be established into a principle, and wrought into a habit. A specific portion of the day must be allotted to it, on which no common engagement must be allowed to intrench.

HANNAH MORE

Into all the world

Until, then, we make our religion a part of our common life, until we bring Christianity... from its retreat to live in the world, and dwell among men; until we have brought it from the closet to the active scene, from the church to the world, whether that world be the court, the senate, the exchange, the public office, the private counting-house, the courts of justice, the professional departments, or the domestic drawing-room, it will not have fully accomplished what it was sent on earth to do.

HANNAH MORE

Advice for women in the world

Dear Children... As to your dressing, I can't believe that there should be any neglect of that beauty God has given you, soe it be done with this caution. As to your conversation, there is nothing fobidden butt what is either prophane, or unjust... 'Tis true, wee should not preach in the Withdrawing roome, butt wee must, by our lookes shew that wee fear God, and that wee dare not hear anything filthy, or that tends to the prejudice of our Neighbour; wee may divert people, and be innocently merry; butt then wee must not please our selves in the thoughts of it... calling to mind that saying of St Paul 'What hast thou which thou didst not receive?' As to your retirement... if you have been faulty... read some Chapter... that doe most divinely sett forth the Love of God to us... that your sorrow for sin may proceed from the sense you have of God's great mercy and love and not from fear of Hell which terrifyes and damnation amazes, and I am never the better for those reflections.

MARGARET BLAGGE

A blessing

What you hold, may you always hold.
What you do, may you always do and never abandon.
But with swift pace, light step,
and unswerving feet,
so that even your steps stir up no dust,
go forward
securely, joyfully, and swiftly,
on the path of prudent happiness,
believing nothing,
agreeing with nothing
which would dissuade you from this resolution
or which would place a stumbling block for you on the way,
so that you may offer your vows to the Most High
in the pursuit of that perfection
to which the Spirit of the Lord has called you.

CLARE OF ASSISI

Nothing is too small for God

In my ninth year... my dear mother took me to London Yearly Meeting... and there for the first time, I had the privilege of listening to that eminent servant of the Lord, Elizabeth Fry. I shall never forget the impression she made upon my young mind by her sweet voice, beautiful face, and her earnest pleading, as she spoke of the prisoners, the suffering and the outcast. I was too young to understand one half of what she said, yet good seed was sowed then and there which led to active labour in after years. In the solemn silence that followed after she took her seat, my childish heart was lift in the prayer that I might grow as good as she was, and work in the same way...

I expressed to my mother a fear that God would not care for a little child like me. She replied by lifting me up to see a bird's nest in the hedgerow, and explaining to me that God taught the little bird to build its nest, and to rear its young; and then bade me pluck a little flower at my feet, and pointed out how nothing was so small to escape his notice...

ELIZABETH L. COMSTOCK

Women's work

No person will deny the importance attached to the character and conduct of a woman, in all her domestic and social relations, when she is filling the station of a daughter, a wife, a mother, or a mistress of a family. But it is a dangerous error to suppose that the duties of females end here. Their gentleness, their natural sympathy with the afflicted, their quickness of discernment, their openness to religious impressions, are points of character (not unusually to be found in our sex) which evidently qualify them, within their own peculiar province, for a far more extensive field of usefulness.

In endeavouring to direct the attention of the female part of society to such objects of Christian charity as they are most calculated to benefit, I may now observe that no persons appear to me to possess so strong a claim on their compassion, and on their pious exertions, as the helpless, the ignorant, the afflicted, or the depraved, of their own sex. It is almost needless to remark, that a multitude of such persons may be found in many of our public institutions.

I rejoice to see the day in which so many women of every rank, instead of spending their time in trifling and unprofitable pursuits, are engaged in works of usefulness and charity. Earnestly is it to be desired that the number of these valuable labourers in the cause of virtue and humanity may be increased, and that all of us may be made sensible of the infinite importance of redeeming the time, of turning our talents to account, and of becoming the faithful, humble, devoted followers of a crucified Lord, who went about DOING GOOD.

ELIZABETH FRY

Faith and life

Those who are interested in reading about having babies do not expect to turn the page and find themselves up against a lot of holy talk. Those who are interested in reading about God do not expect to have to wade through a heap of dirty nappies to get there. But to keep life and religion apart in such a way is false to both sides. More and more persistently, theologians throughout the world are calling for an experience-based theology. They know that if faith does not spring out of and return to the ground soil of daily existence, then it means nothing. Faith needs life to find its true nature.

At the same time life needs faith. The strong emotions aroused by motherhood and the everyday slog of bringing up children find their true meaning as part of a relationship with God.

MARGARET HEBBLETHWAITE

Keeping on

Wherever we are there are small situations going wrong, and we are to redeem them, but if we start on the way of redemption and refuse when it begins to make us suffer, whether it is our pride, or our nerves, or our comfort, we are most horribly disloyal.

FLORENCE ALLSHORN

Only channels

When Jesus tells us to love our enemies, He Himself will give us the love with which to do it. We are neither factories nor reservoirs of His love, only channels. When we understand that, all excuse for pride is eliminated.

CORRIE TEN BOOM

The results are not important

You say to me, 'There are so few who really profit by all our work'... I say to you, 'It does not matter!' Let us go on sowing the seed just the same. Give of your best even if only a very few profit. It would be satisfying to see results, but it is not results that are important... Let us do what we can and God will do the rest.

JULIE BILLIART

Careful with that plumbline!

If you feel strong and correct, look out! If you go about trying to set others straight according to your plumbline, God help you! And God help the others you are trying to 'help'.

One woman wrote, 'My mother is a marvellous woman, but she is right about everything! I love her, but I simply can't live in the house with her and neither can my sister.'

Only God is right about everything. Only God's plumbline falls straight, and only He has a right to use it.

EUGENIA PRICE

Giving from a distance

[T]hey are only too willing to give from a distance... to have sickness and misery... kept out of sight... decontaminated. Their unexamined motive is not to heal suffering but to disinfect it.

CARYLL HOUSELANDER

Love like Jesus'

We knew well enough in theory that the love that Jesus Christ had said was to be like His own does not start like that, that it does not start with the romantic love of the poets but with the very unpoetical neighbour. There was a difference between the thing we had known as friendship and this all-embracing friendliness which Christ epitomized in His own life.

FLORENCE ALLSHORN

We do not love

When you add to love of God and neighbour, love of our enemies, the difficulty becomes acute…

That we love is one of the illusions we moderns most cherish about ourselves. We will admit cheerfully that we are not 'strictly' truthful, that we are lazy, greedy, self-indulgent, proud, angry (though we prefer to say righteously indignant), that we take the Lord's name in vain and profane the Sabbath, but all these minor sins, we imply, are amply compensated for by the way we love. 'I love people', we say frequently, complacently, and as conventionally as the pious used to boast that they were saved by grace.

Yet obviously we do not love, or the world would not be what it is to-day. We do not love vividly enough even to avoid conflicts among those who seriously wish to get along together and accomplish good works.

Wrangles in committees, acrimonious disputes over the phrasing of resolutions, hard feelings among leaders in women's auxiliaries are only a few items of evidence that even when we are consciously about the Lord's business we do not love. When we encounter people of opposing politics, different races or economic theories, when we meet with opponents who quite openly do not care whether they reach agreement or not so long as they get what they want, our bankruptcy of love proclaims itself in the feuds, persecutions, discriminations, wars and chaos of our times.

'Love and do what you will,' said St Augustine, but he did not mean, as we seem to interpret it, to pretend to love and be as bad as you want to be. He meant, if you really love, you cannot do ill; all the things that you wish to do, informed by your love, will be beneficient.

Love, powerful, healing, quickening, enduring, the bond of peace and of all virtues, is of God. We cannot constrain it of our own effort, but we can have it as a gift from Him, if we want it enough, if we pray for it urgently, unceasingly. Pour it into our hearts, in a generous, life-giving flood, for we have sore need of it.

ELIZABETH GRAY VINING

I give you

Lord Jesus:
I give you my hands, to do your work.
I give you my feet, to go your way.
I give you my eyes, to see as you do.
I give you my tongue, to speak your words.
I give you my mind, that you may think in me.
I give you my spirit, that you may pray in me.
Above all, I give you my heart,
that you may love in me your Father and all mankind.
I give you my whole self, that you may grow in me.
So that it is you, Lord Jesu,
Who lives and works and prays in me.

THE GRAIL SOCIETY

Stir me!

Two students claimed to know something of painting, so were dispatched with two brushes and a one-gallon tin of white hard-gloss paint, to tackle the window, door and blackboard frames in each room of the school...

Moving round inspecting all the different areas of work, I went in search of the painters to see how they were faring... I looked at the woodwork round the door... I touched it gingerly. There was a sort of brown, sticky 'goo'... I strode across to them, and looked into the paint pot.

There was a solid mass of white matter, under a very thin remaining layer of rapidly disappearing linseed oil. The pot had not been stirred... I demonstrated the art of stirring. Hard work, right down to the bottom of the can, till all that was solid was stirred into the diluting oil, to become one consistency... Some half an hour later, I suddenly realized that I had failed to explain that the paint would need stirring every so often until the job was completed... .

The next morning, being at heart a teacher, I gave the morning Bible study on the subject of 'stirring': how we as Christians need to let God stir us, right down to the bottom of our innermost beings. Paul had said: 'I put thee in remembrance that thou *stir up* the gift of God, which is in thee...' (2 Timothy 1:6), and I wanted to help each student ask God to stir him deeply. We needed to be stirred until there was no separation left between solid and liquid, between secular and spiritual, weekdays and Sundays. Our lives needed to be of one consistency, through and through, ready to do the task for which we were created. This stirring would need to be continued daily until the task was completed. At the close of our Bible study, one of the students prayed in French, the Government language, rather haltingly:

'Go ahead, God, stir me. I don't care what it costs...': then there was a long pause, before he burst out, in his mother tongue: 'I do care what it costs, I care a lot, but stir me all the same, O God!'

How my mind snapped back to Keswick, over twenty years before. That was the prayer of my heart, and has been ever since.

'Stir me, dear God, to live for You in the very fullest sense, by the faith of Your dear Son, our Saviour Jesus Christ. Stir me, that I may step out of the apathy and indifference and lethargy that seek to overwhelm our modern society, in self-sufficiency and self-complacency. Stir me to move out into the exciting realm of faith, to see Jesus Christ at work through me in all the daily details of living. Give me the courage to believe and to act in faith.'

HELEN ROSEVEARE

Go deep

What was Jesus saying when he told the fishermen to go deeper before they let down their nets?

Perhaps that relying on shallow, surface resources will not be enough for authentic living, and that—within a discipline of stillness and trust—we must let down our defences and delve deep into the resources of God. Then we might be able to chance the impossible.

Perhaps, too, he was saying that there are no quick fixes in the missionary enterprise… that we must enter deeply into the lives—the joys, wounds, fears and dreams—of people, in order to be Christ to them in their situation. A redemptive involvement with one another is a deep and self-sacrificial involvement.

Thus his words have implications for both prayer and action. When we 'pray deep', we will be able to 'live deep'.

KATE COMPSTON

Where the action is

The Gospel of Peace

The experience of sharing the lives of the poor in my community in Africa shook me out of my complacency and insensitivity to injustice happening all around me at home. On my return to England, my eyes were opened for the first time. I saw men and women who had no homes lining up in queues for soup at day centres, whilst in the streets, people walking aimlessly with blank, lifeless expressions on their faces are those whose self esteem and purpose in life has been eroded by long-term unemployment.

Yet at the same time the Government in my name spends billions of pounds on weapons systems intending to destroy millions of people—each person created by the God who created me. I ask myself over again, 'How can I have been oblivious to the stock piling of nuclear weapons in this country? How can I all these years have failed to grasp the point of Christ's Gospel of Peace?'

MARGARET HOLDEN

Children—the real VIPs

In the last few years cases of child abuse have seemed to be growing in number, whether because of a greater awareness or that they occur more often; but it is evil and tragic, and a very sad reflection on life today. The words of Jesus are as clear and firm today as when he spoke them while here on earth two thousand years ago. Children are a precious gift to be cared for, to be honoured and protected. They have a God-given right to enjoy their innocence and must be allowed and encouraged to discover and grow in freedom, a freedom that also protects and shelters them from anything and anyone that would hurt, maim or pervert them.

Thank God for those who have taken seriously to heart the command of Jesus to care for little ones. Thank God for their faithfulness and love. Do we, though, see the care of children as a priority in our church or community? Do we do anything for them personally? I know how difficult it is to get people to teach in Sunday school, run youth clubs, even give a hand in the creche. I hear the grumbles of good Christian people when a child cries during a service, or when a couple of toddlers decide to go and play games in the aisle. I know my own feelings when the noise level goes above what I consider acceptable. I get edgy and selfishly wish the parents would take them out. ... Yet my greatest joys have been when those same little folk have been brought up for a blessing,... when they so trustingly run up to me, for they have completely forgotten I had glared or tut-tutted at them; and I am thankful to them for giving me another chance. These are the real VIPs... They have so much to teach me about love and acceptance, about forgiveness and the joy of living each moment to the full. I just pray I may not get too old to learn!

MARGARET CUNDIFF

Carrying God's message

Sometimes I'm asked if I feel I have a mission. I don't. I'm not that presumptuous. I don't think God looked down and said 'Here's Betty Bloomer*, we're going to use her to sober up alcoholics.' But I do think people relate to someone who has the same problems they have, and who overcomes them. And I think God has allowed me—along with thousands of others— to carry a message that says, there's help out there, and you too can be a survivor. Look at us. Look at me.

BETTY FORD (WHOSE MAIDEN NAME WAS BLOOMER*)

Harvest festival

We offer to you,
Swordless Lord,
those who have perished
by the sword.
We offer our harvest festival,
the barren earth,
the yield of blood,
sown in the potter's field.
At least, not a lie
in your presence, Lord.
We offer ourselves
and the waste of our conquering,
we who have lived
and died
by the sword.

CARYLL HOUSELANDER (WRITTEN 10 AUGUST 1945)

Strong enough love

It seems to me that what matters is to create in this world a force of love strong enough to combat that of hate—and more particularly of fear… I do so agree with you that the official hate propaganda is one of the greatest tragedies of war. And there ought to be a continual quiet resistance of it. There is not room for love and hate in one heart.

CARYLL HOUSELANDER

Prayer alone

After the war what will have happened to the mind under the tin hat?… Now is the time to prepare defences for the mind… *The first is prayer*… Prayer alone can teach us to concentrate again… make our minds ready for other essential things… for the contemplation (not merely observation) of beauty.

CARYLL HOUSELANDER

Special Sunday

One of the great sadnesses I personally feel is the loss of Sunday. It has been gradually eroded away until we are left with a day like any other day of the week when people rush frantically around, getting nowhere fast. A backlash against the Victorian Sunday, maybe, but the God-given gift of a day of rest was intended for our good, body, mind and spirit. The human frame cannot go on day after day, week after week, without regular breaks, a release from work and routine. The mind cannot continue to cope with the burdens we place on it, while the spiritual side shrivels, dies, and the wholeness of life that God intended for us is put out of joint, and deformed, and we all suffer. I look forward to Sunday. It is for me a heaven-sent opportunity to share with others, to have time to spend in God's house and with his people, to be free from the demands of the week, to be able to relax, to breathe, to be.

MARGARET CUNDIFF

Solidarity with the poor

It is tempting for us to rush into singing the songs of the oppressed as if we could indeed quite simply make their words our own. Sometimes we can, but not simply. We should feel uneasy with a lusty singing of the triumph songs of the poor, when we have no right to triumphalism, given where we are standing and whose side we are in fact on. To pretend that we *are* the poor may give us the feeling of occupying the high moral ground we naively assume is theirs; but it doesn't assist either worship or action because it is untruthful.

Much harder, but in the end more hopeful, is to seek solidarity with the poor. Solidarity means truthfully recognizing the place we stand in, while really seeing theirs; and then, with love and honesty and commitment, exploring the connections between us and working together for change. For us, it will mean facing the complexity and ambivalence of where we are placed, as Christians living in the rich world who want to pray in solidarity with the poor. It will entail acknowledging both our participation in sin and our own woundedness. It will require repentance (*metanoia*—a change of stance in relation to the evil that seeks to surround us). But it will also release us to share in a passionate desire for change in the structures of the world— *for our sake too*. We will recognize a struggle and find joy, forgiveness, and salvation as we join it. The poor ask not for patronage but solidarity: 'if you have come to help me, then you are wasting your time. But if you have come because your liberation is bound up with mine, then let us work together' (Lilla Watson, Australian Aboriginal).

JANET MORLEY

What good is freedom?

I'm not a heroine. I love freedom and would very much like to be free now with my family and friends. But I can't buy freedom at any price; I don't want to act against my conscience. I love freedom, but what good is freedom to me if I can't call God my Father?... The knowledge that my soul and thoughts are free encourages and strengthens me.

AIDA SKRIPNIKOVA

Reverence for things

The relation between us and THINGS is not to be despised. They are entitled to a measure of reverence not only because of their origin, but because they may at any moment be used for God to speak to us by. Perhaps we miss urgent messages by ignoring the sacramental language of the everyday modern world... Perhaps we are not only depriving ourselves, but also failing to put into the material world the spiritual content it needs. It is not only Nature, the Creation, which in Paul's words is waiting for the revealing of the sons of God; this whole complex world-wide network of twentieth-century civilisation is waiting to be blessed by those whose minds are 'set to hallow all they find'.

MARY F. SMITH

Liberation theology

I talked with catechists and priests in refugee camps and slums, with a Lutheran bishop and a Jesuit professor, with mothers and wives of the missing—talked about the suffering servant of God while talking about the poor. They spoke from an inner power which the Bible calls the 'strength in weakness,' the 'hope against hope,' the 'great joy among the poor.' I must confess that I did not fully understand and that I often resist this with the rational, economic, and psychological tools with which my culture has equipped me...

What I understand is that there is a spirituality which does not permit us to define life through money and power, a spirit of courage, strength, and joy which does not submit to this central definition of our culture—money and might. What I do not understand is where the joy comes from, the struggle and the solidarity, or the certainty of the poor that God is with them. What I do not understand is the mystery of God; it is the fire which I, a doubting woman in Europe overwhelmed by the shadows, often think can be extinguished.

And with that I arrive at the gift of the poor to the depressive rich, at the *teologia de la liberacion*... The theology of liberation is one of the great gifts of the poor of Latin America to Christianity, as well as to the middle class of the rich world, to which I belong. It is a gift which is not used up; it nourishes me, as it nourishes the poor.

'And the bush was blazing, yet it was not consumed.' This is how I experience the pictures, the prayers, the biblical interpretation, the belief of this theology. It represents a gift to the world church, even if the latter has not yet grasped it. ...

The various forms of Christianity—orthodoxy, liberalism, and liberation theology—are still wrestling with one another. But we can recognize the signs of liberation: the blind begin to see, the lame begin to walk, and the poor are given back their dignity. The God of the poor appears, and in this epiphany of God the Christian religion unfolds its revolutionary strength. This religion, which for many in the First World was sterile, incomprehensible folderol, a straitjacket of hypocritical morality, an outdated opium of the people which had meanwhile long since been replaced by psychology as the new opium of the middle class—this religion is alive in the new social movements for peace, justice and the integrity of creation.

The poor are the teachers, according to a basic principle of liberation theology. What do they teach me then, when the gap between my technology, knowledge, money, and power and theirs is unbridgeable? How have they then 'evangelized' me, how have they converted me, what have they given me?...

The most important thing I have learned from the power I recognize in the losing battles in which we are involved here at home. To be sure, we analyze how the financial elite continue to produce hunger and poverty, but who wants to hear it? To be sure, we fight against every new war toy which our masters consider necessary and profitable, but the militarization not only of our country but of our brains continues to advance. Many let themselves be dealt with by tear gas and clubs in order to save at least a part of this creation.

In all these struggles the greatest danger for us lies in becoming tired and giving up, letting ourselves be diverted or corrupted, falling into dependence on drugs, alcohol, or prosperity, becoming depoliticized because we submit ourselves to the idol of oppression, who whispers to us with a soft voice: 'Nothing can be done about it.'

From the poor of Latin America I learn their hope, their toughness, their anger and their patience. I learn a better theology in which God is not Lord-over-us but Strength-in-us. In which the miracles of Jesus are not distinguished from ours; we too drive out demons and heal the sick. I learn trust in the people of God. I overcome skepticism, false conciliatoriness, and short-sighted illusory hopes. I practice betrayal of my own class. I leave their spiritual apartheid and move towards the liberation of all. I gain a part; I belong to them. I am less alone. I begin to hunger and thirst after righteousness. I am evangelized, and I sing along from the new person:

Creadores de la historia,
constructores de nueva humanidad.

DOROTHEE SOELLE

Real life

Some of us were good at taking prayers, others at talking in study groups, others at practical work, but it was in none of these things as such, it was in the actual attitude and deed over a saucepan, or in your quality of thinking of someone else, whether you took sides or healed the separation between sides that was the actual test. You can sit in your principal's room, or before your class, and talk with real earnestness, but the great things are not won like that. Humility, generosity, peace-making only rise from the actually controlled deed, the love-restrained re-action, the detached from self sight of truth in a situation in which the truth is not pleasant for you. In the actual working together you have to change your natural self-guarding laziness and carelessness if you are to live at peace. The adventures are endless and it is a continual actual choosing whether you go the way of self or the way of love. You cannot cover over what you are by any amount of brilliant talk, even spiritual talk. We could talk in the chapel without the guilt of hypocrisy only as we lived in the house.

FLORENCE ALLSHORN

Sweeping statement

In the same chapter as we read about the Good Shepherd, we also read that God is like a woman sweeping for a lost coin. I know nothing about sheep, and a lot about sweeping, but I've never yet seen a woman sweeping, in a stained glass window.

LOIS WILSON

Messengers

It suddenly strikes me
with overwhelming force:
It was women
who were first to spread the message of Easter—
the unheard of!
It was women
who rushed to the disciples,
who, breathless and bewildered,
passed on the greatest message of all:
He is alive!
Think if women had kept silence
in the churches!

MARTA WILHELMSON

Christ for the world

When I saw and laughed at the oversized American pants sent as relief goods, I realized that I, too, might be doing the same thing: bringing an 'over-sized unfit' Jesus in the Immaculate Host to an uncomprehending people. Not that I don't appreciate Jesus in the Eucharist, but that having focussed perhaps too much attention on the Host, I failed to encounter Him alive in the tribals. After all, did I bring Jesus there, or was He not there already, waiting for me?

A SISTER FROM BUIKIDNON

Got any bread?

Real evangelism is one beggar telling another beggar where to find bread!

ROSALIND RINKER

Multi-racial England

Mrs T, who reminds me so much of that old widow Anna, who, in Luke's account of the presentation of the Christ child in the Temple, became the first evangelist, sharing with her neighbours the joy of having seen the Lord. Mrs T is one of the few white members left in our congregation. She must have been there for many long years, since the days when it was a flourishing suburban church, full of missionary zeal. Then came the war and the bombs and the rebuilding, and the subsequent flight to the newer suburbs as local families moved out and the immigrants moved in. But Mrs T stayed, loyal to her church even as she watched it changing beyond all recognition. As familiar figures passed on or moved away, she would always be there in her same familiar place, praying that one day the empty seats around her would be filled again and that God would raise up new leaders to fill the vacant offices.

Today her prayers have been abundantly answered as she is surrounded by new friends, people whom she loves and who love her with such warm affection that there seems no such thing as racial barriers or generation gaps. As she said to me one day, 'We used to sing at our missionary meetings,

"Coming, coming, yes they are,
Coming, coming from afar"

and now they have come, from the Caribbean, and from Africa, and from Asia. How fortunate I am to have lived to see this day and to enjoy their company!'

PAULINE WEBB

Married or unmarried

I don't think it makes any difference whether you are married or unmarried. Whether you are married or unmarried is a circumstance within the Christian life. If you are married, you have a special task, if you are unmarried you have something else to do. Both have a different witness to give. I think the married home can be one of the greatest witnesses you can make these days, because there are so many unhappy marriages, so much misery. In being married you can redeem the word marriage and make it something beautiful again. On the other hand, I think the unmarried person has something very fine to do, in showing that without having anything the world says you must have if you are going to be happy, you can still be happy and fulfilled, and I am very glad I have been able to prove that true. I had no parents since the age of three. I never had any money, never had any future, I tried to be an artist and couldn't, I never had a husband or children, yet I am as happy as anybody I know. I am really fulfilled. So I do not think it matters.

FLORENCE ALLSHORN

Family or household?

In New Testament times, the household existed in Hebrew, Greek and Roman societies as a voluntary association of parents, children, servants and other dependents for their mutual benefit. It is not surprising that the household played an important role in the growth and stability of the first churches… Whereas the household can be composed of misfits and outcasts, the family—whether nuclear or extended—excludes people who do not belong. Thus the popular concept of the local church as a family is based on its exclusiveness. It is time for western Christians to abandon the idolatry of the family and to explore the implications of the biblical metaphors of the Household of God and the Household of Faith.

MARION BEALES

PART FOUR

Time to rejoice

Women of Spirit rejoice, they praise God, trying—and not always succeeding—to praise Him in all circumstances. They see the sunshine, take holidays, relax, have fun, make mistakes, celebrate Christmas. Don't you? So here are joyous things, happy stories to share. Good news.

Renascence

For two years
The great cat,
Imagination,
Slept on.
Then suddenly
The other day
What had lain dormant
Woke
To a shower
A proliferation
Of images.
My Himalayan cat
Sits on the terrace wall
Back to the sea
His blue eyes wide open
Alive to every stir of a leaf
Every wing in the air
And I recognize him
As a mage.
After long silence
An old poet
Singing again,
I am a mage myself
Joy leaps in my throat.
Glory be to God!

MAY SARTON

Open the doors

For more than a year I tried to persuade myself that I could not possibly go to China. 'Lord,' I said finally, 'if you really want me to go, send me a sign. Open the doors before me.'

And sure enough, much to my surprise, I did earn enough to buy the train ticket; I was granted a passport; I did learn of a lady missionary who needed an assistant. A few months later I was bouncing along in a third-class, trans-continental train.

GLADYS AYLWARD

Home sweet home

We have grown up with a Christianity that has little room for the physical both in terms of human bodies and in terms of places to put them. Our thinkers and guides have for centuries been men without a wife and family, and without a home unless it be a monastery. Yes, if it comes to a monastery we have learnt to find the sacred in it. Monasteries are places that speak to us of God just by walking around them. But we have not learnt to relate to the sacred in the family home, so that just by walking around the house of a Christian family we can feel we are drinking in draughts of God. We have not dared to think in those terms...

MARGARET HEBBLETHWAITE

Celebrating Christmas

There is no time in the Christian year when the home is more important than Christmas. Christmas is the time to adorn your house, fill it with the food of celebration, and invite those who are alone to come in and share it with you...

[T]he place where a new-born baby belongs is at home. A stable had to do once, but it is not where anyone would choose, and as we remember Jesus' birth year after year we prepare our homes for him as we prepare our hearts for him.

No religious feast requires more physical work. Advent is supposed to be a time of meditation and penance, but usually the mother's mortifications are more worldly and more directly linked to the coming celebrations...

Celebrating Christmas can involve an enormous amount of work:... All these things are indeed an advent penance of a real, physical, human kind; they are the way mothers put themselves out to show the importance of Jesus' coming in their lives; the way also in which they have spread the good news to all—to those to whom they have sent cards, to those to whom they have sung carols, to those to whom they have made a donation, to those who pass their house and see their Christmas tree lit up in the window, to those who share in the turkey they cooked and the cake they have made, and most of all to their children for whom more than anyone the work has been done, because the whole of the festivities is a huge educational aid for the simple but life-changing message 'Jesus Christ is born'. At Christmas, mothers take the lead in preaching the gospel.

MARGARET HEBBLETHWAITE

Holiday

Do you know I think one of the best things you can do on holiday is to ask nothing, want nothing, but just praise God for everything. Always be praising Him—for the little sticky leaves, the rich sombre greenness of the trees, all the kindness you get, on a holiday. Just one long praise of little beautiful things and forget that great, big, striving, blundering self of yours. Then come back to us clean and fresh and contagious and let us too get a sight of the glory of God.

FLORENCE ALLSHORN

Acceptance

When Jesus told the man on the pallet that his sins were forgiven he was in effect saying this, 'It is all right to be you. I love you as you are and God loves you as you are. We understand your weakness and vulnerability. There is no need to be afraid and bury yourself under masks because God and I love all those aspects of yourself that you have made into your shadow side, we love the maskless you utterly and unconditionally. So there is no need to be weighted down by guilt, alienation and despair. Be yourself, live your life honestly, openly and fearlessly because we will never reject you. But if you slip back into the shadows do not worry because we are with you in the darkness and want to bring you back into the light.' Forgiveness is the love and acceptance of people as they are.

ELIZABETH STUART

God is there

Any relationship based upon love and acceptance can become sacramental, *ubi caritas et amore, Deus ibi est*—where charity and love are found, God himself is there.

ELIZABETH STUART

Give thanks

On the very night before they crucified Him, Jesus 'took the cup and gave thanks.' Things were not going well for Him that night! But He gave thanks anyway.

Gratitude was the normal state of His heart.

If your life is good, if things are going well for you, if your cup is running over, don't stop with a fleeting period of guilt for not having been thankful enough. No point in wasting time with that. Simply begin to give thanks. Give thanks if your cup is filled with sweetness and drink it with grace. Give thanks also if your cup is only half-full or even filled with trouble, and drink it with grace. Grace is available for us under all conditions. Grace to give thanks to our Father. The grace Jesus Christ brings into the human life is never limited by the circumstances of that life.

EUGENIA PRICE

Begin...

Ingratitude snaps shut the human heart. Grateful hearts are always open hearts. They are hearts which have received. Even God cannot squeeze a blessing through a closed heart.

We need to form the habit of *gratitude*. It can change everything!... One little start towards being grateful to God for health, for food, for His love, begins at once to make us feel less *inferior*. If He cares enough to give us these things—maybe we have been exaggerating our pitiable plight! An ungrateful heart is a blind heart. It cannot see its blessings until it begins to give thanks.

EUGENIA PRICE

Bathed in light

Childbirth is a peak experience, but not a lying one, not a brief moment of success in a miserable, hopeless world that will soon swallow it up. It is a privileged moment, God-given for our learning, so that remembering what we then saw so clearly our whole lives after may be bathed in light.

MARGARET HEBBLETHWAITE

Ah, Mary we hardly know you

Ah, Mary we hardly know you—
A few tantalizing glimpses
relegated by most to 'introduction'
useful to lead into the 'real' story,
relegated to the task and place of women—
standing by and watching over,
caring for needs,
keeping a death watch,
providing loving care
for the body of the dead one,
the child of your womb.
Ah, Mary we discover you—
One who was open and receptive—
open to the love and mercy of God,
open to embodiment of the living word,
receptive to life,
you became filled with life.
Ah, Mary you have become the glory of God—
'The glory of God is a human being fully alive.'
You are the glory of God!
Ah, Mary we hardly knew you—
A few tantalizing glimpses
but we look at you afresh
and in you begin to see ourselves.
We are the dwelling place of God.
We are the glory of God.
Thanks be to God!

KAREN SUMMERS

My angel

I have only ever seen an angel once. It was on a rainy day, when I was eight years old. I had been kept indoors all morning, but at last the clouds cleared a little, the rain stopped and I went out to play. No one was about, so I filled the time waiting for my friends by throwing a ball up against the side of the house. Then I looked up and saw the angel—high above me, robed in white, haloed in gold and floating across a sky that had suddenly cleared to a violet blue. I ran to call my mother to come and see my angel. She was busy and had no time to come just at that moment, but she said, 'You are very lucky to see that angel. Not many people see them. I expect if I came I would see only a cloud, edged with sunshine in a rainy sky. But you have seen an angel.' 'What is an angel?' I asked her. 'It really means a messenger of God,' she said, 'and God sends messages to us in many ways. Your angel is telling you what a beautiful place the world can be, even on a rainy day.'

PAULINE WEBB

A message

If I have any message to leave, it is this: Believe in God. He guides and protects you all through life, as I trust this account of my life has demonstrated. Discipline yourself daily by having a plan—not just vague, wishful thinking. Commit yourself daily to doing something, however small, for somebody else, for by making other people happy you will find true happiness yourself.

OLAVE, LADY BADEN-POWELL

Hate into love

I saw [my own mother] regularly, but it was always as though there was a glass wall between her and me. I prayed a great deal about what I recognized as my coldness of heart, superiority and criticism—but nothing changed.

[Then] a friend asked me a question... 'Why have you never made a home for your mother?'... I am grateful to remember, she persisted and at intervals twice more repeated the question. The third time I really blew up. To my own surprise I heard myself say with great violence, 'If you think I'd make a home for the woman who abandoned me as a baby, you are wrong!'...

My wise friend... said, 'The way you spoke was very real. Why don't you take time alone with God and ask Him to show you the truth?' So I went home and did just that. For a time my mind was in a turmoil, then one devastatingly clear thought came. 'You hate your mother.' It came with blinding truth... I could only admit that it was true and that I had no idea what to do about it. If I was completely honest, I didn't really want to do anything about it, except to be free of the sense of guilt. But I also told God that I knew it was utterly wrong. I don't think that until then I had ever understood what was meant by 'being saved'. I did then, for I knew that I needed saving from something far beyond any power of mine to cope with. Now the truth was out and I found myself literally shaking with hate. The thought of seeing my mother was almost intolerable. Then God spoke to me again: 'If you will do what I tell you, I will deal with your hate.'...

My mother by now was in a home in Sussex, having had a stroke. My thought was to let my flat, and go and live near her for as long as her life should last. This was the cross for me, for it cut across all I wanted to do, and I knew that, short of a miracle, I could never give her the love and care she so badly needed at this time of her life. But when I acted, God opened the way. I understood the miracle on the Damascus road.

Suddenly He turned my hate to love. Suddenly I knew that everything had changed... I found a home with a friend nearby and was able to visit my mother as often as I liked. She had a second stroke which left her physically helpless, but her mind clear... She lived for six months and we had rich and happy times together... In very truth we became mother and daughter.

One Sunday, after a particularly happy afternoon in which she said what it had meant to her to have me with her, she died—swiftly and peacefully. As I looked at her face with its happy little smile, I thanked God from the bottom of my heart for His love and goodness; for the miracle of forgiveness, the power that changes character, dissolves bitterness and builds eternal unity. I was so grateful that I had obeyed the thought that came as I was leaving her room that Sunday—to go back and give her another kiss and tell her how much I loved her. 'Darling,' was her reply, 'I don't know what I'd have done without you these last months.'

JOAN PORTER BUXTON

God understands

God is not malicious. Not punitive. Not a trickster. Not out to play jokes on us. God may ask us to wait longer than we want, but only if waiting is in our best interests.

God knows our hearts and God understands our healing needs. God understands the good that is waiting around the corner for us, the good that we can't see yet. God sees the benefit in the lessons we're learning, not just the turmoil, which is what we so often focus on.

God can help us bring out the healer in ourselves.

MELODY BEATTIE

Say thank you

Gratitude has immense tranformational powers—for ourselves, our lives, and our circumstances. I have used this tool over and over again. It has taken me through many stressful circumstances—poverty, divorce, being alone, learning how to date, moves, overwhelming projects, overwhelming feelings, troubles with children, troubles with neighbours, fear, circumstances that perplexed me, and other unlit, foggy parts of this journey. Gratitude helps make things work out well. It helps us feel better while stressful things are happening. Then when things get better, it helps us enjoy the good...

Force gratitude. Say thank you again and again for each circumstance. Say thank you even if you're not feeling grateful. Eventually the power of gratitude will take over, and joy and true gratitude will begin.

MELODY BEATTIE

Enjoy!

It seems to me that the very great thing is to be able to enjoy life. When I was in the hospital last year and they told me... that they were not at all sure that they could operate, I felt no fear of death, though I did not want to die... But what I *did* feel was remorse because I realized that I had never really *let* myself *enjoy* life—so many scruples and inhibitions and things preventing me from really enjoying the sheer loveliness of the world, the people in it, and even the material things in it, food, drink, the sun, spending money, etc... I made only one resolution: if I was given another chance (as I have been), I would enjoy everything in life that I can, for as long as I can, and as wholly as I can.

CARYLL HOUSELANDER

Little things

To those who may feel that I ascribe to faith such simple events, such small happenings, I would say that life is mainly made up of little things, but that the fact that they are little does not make them unimportant. Faith can remove molehills as well as mountains, and only by practising faith continually in the seemingly insignificant things does one develop the power to overcome the big crises when they come. I have learnt that the true practice of faith is really a state of being, a state in which one is unwaveringly expectant of good, and in which one thanks God for benefits before they are actually manifest.

KATIE WHITELEGG

Can God still perform miracles?

One night I had worked hard to help a mother in the labour ward, but despite all we could do, she died, leaving us with a tiny premature baby, and a crying two-year-old daughter. We would have difficulty in keeping the baby alive, as we had no incubator (we had no electricity to run an incubator!) and no special feeding facilities. Despite living on the equator, nights were often chilly, with treacherous draughts. One pupil midwife went for the box we used for such babies, and the cotton wool they were wrapped in. Another went to stoke up the fire and fill a hot water bottle. She came back shortly, in distress, to tell me that, in filling the bottle, it had burst. Rubber perishes easily in tropical climates.

'And it is our last hot water bottle!' she exclaimed.

As in the west, it is no good crying over spilt milk, so in Central Africa it might be considered no good crying over burst hot water bottles. They do not grow on trees, and there are no chemist stores down forest pathways.

'All right,' I said, 'Put the baby as near the fire as you safely can: sleep between the baby and the door to keep it free from draughts. Your job is to keep the baby warm.'

The following midday, I went to have prayers with any of the orphanage children who chose to gather with me, as I did most days. I gave the youngsters various suggestions of things to pray about, and told them about the tiny baby. I explained our problem about keeping the baby warm enough, mentioning the burst hot water bottle. The baby could so easily die if it got chilled. I also told them of the two-year-old sister, crying because her mother had died.

During prayer time, one ten-year-old girl, Ruth, prayed, with the usual blunt conciseness of our African children.

'Please, God,' she prayed, 'send us a hot water bottle. It'll be no good tomorrow, God, as the baby'll be dead, so please send it this afternoon.'

While I gasped inwardly at the audacity of the prayer, she added, by way of corollary: 'And while You are about it, would You please send a dolly for the little girl, so she'll know You really love her?'

As often with the children's prayers, I was put on the spot. Could I honestly say 'Amen'? I just did not believe that God could do this. Oh, yes, I know that he can do everything. The Bible says so. But there are limits, aren't there? And I had some very big 'buts'. The only way God *could* answer this particular prayer would be by sending me a parcel from the homeland. I had been in Africa almost four years at that time, and I had never, never received a parcel from home: and anyway, if anyone *did* send me a parcel, who would put in a hot water bottle? I lived on the equator!

Halfway through the afternoon... a message was sent that there was a car at my front door. By the time I reached home, the car had gone, but there, on the verandah, was a large 22lb (10kg) parcel, all done up with paper and string, and bearing U.K. stamps. I felt tears pricking my eyes. I could not open the parcel alone, so I sent for the orphanage children...

From the top, I lifted out brightly coloured, knitted jerseys. Eyes sparkled as I gave them out. Then there were knitted bandages for the leprosy patients and they looked a little bored. Then a large bar of soap—and the children were probably more bored! Then a box of mixed raisins and sultanas—that would make a nice batch of buns for the weekend. Then, as I put my hand in again, I felt the... could it really be? I grasped it and pulled it out—yes, a brand-new rubber hot water bottle! I cried. I had not asked God to send it: I had not truly believed that He could.

Ruth was in the front row of the children. She rushed forward, crying out: 'If God has sent the bottle, He must have sent the dolly too!'

Rummaging down to the bottom of the box, she pulled out the small, beautifully dressed dolly. Her eyes shone! She had never doubted...

That parcel had been on the way five whole months. Packed up by my old GCU class, the leader had heard and obeyed God's prompting to send a hot water bottle, even to the equator: and one of the girls had put in a dolly for an African child—five months before—in answer to the believing prayer of a ten-year-old, to bring it 'that afternoon'. Can God still perform miracles? Is He the same yesterday, today and for ever—in Israel, Africa and anywhere else—where He finds living faith? Indeed He can and is!

HELEN ROSEVEARE

And the last shall be first

Jesus said to the two Marys: 'All hail!' And they came and held him by the feet, and worshipped him. Then said Jesus unto them, 'Be not afraid: go, tell my brethren that they go into Galilee, and there shall they see me' (Matthew 28:9, 10). There are two or three points in this beautiful narrative to which we wish to call the attention of our readers.

First, it was the first announcement of the glorious news to a lost world and a company of forsaking disciples. Second, it was as public as the nature of the case demanded; and intended ultimately to be published to the ends of the earth. Third, Mary was expressly commissioned to reveal the fact to the apostles; and thus she literally became their teacher on that memorable occasion. Oh, glorious privilege, to be allowed to herald the glad tidings of a Saviour risen! How could it be that our Lord chose a woman to this honour? Well, one reason might be that the male disciples were all missing at the time. They all forsook him, and fled. But woman was there, as she had ever been, ready to minister to her risen, as to her dying, Lord.

> Not she with traitorous lips her Saviour stung,
> Not she denied him with unholy tongue;
> She, whilst apostles shrunk, could danger brave;
> Last at the cross, and earliest at the grave.

But, surely, if the dignity of our Lord or his message were likely to be imperilled by committing this sacred trust to a woman, he who was guarded by legions of angels could have commanded another messenger; but, as if intent on doing her honour, and rewarding her unwavering fidelity, he reveals himself first to her; and, as an evidence that he had taken out of the way the curse under which she had so long groaned, nailing it to his cross, he makes her who had been first in the transgression first also in the glorious knowledge of complete redemption.

CATHERINE BOOTH

The golden thread

When I was about seven years old, I announced that my favourite text was 'Hitherto hath the Lord helped me'. The elders were amused, but I am not so sure that it was funny after all. The distance from one birthday to the next seems infinite to a small child, and 'the thoughts of youth are long long thoughts.' Looking back over many years, I fancy my choice now would be much the same. I am not prepared, here and now, to analyse and define the reasons, but I can only say that this quiet certainty has run all through my life, linking up babyhood and youth and middle age with the latest stretch of the road... and 'hitherto', though sometimes almost slipping through one's fingers, that golden thread has never wholly escaped my grasp.

ELIZABETH FOX HOWARD

Even in Hell...

There is no need for anyone to press upon me the reality of Hell as the early Calvinists did with stoney hearts, for I have been in Hell, but having been there myself, I am driven to believe that there is Love below all.

JOSEPHINE BUTLER

Look forward

The coming of the Kingdom is perpetual—the real Christian is
always a revolutionary—God is with the future.

EVELYN UNDERHILL

Biographical information

(SELECTED CONTRIBUTORS)

Sylvia Mary Alison

Sylvia Mary Alison is the founder of the Prison Fellowship in England and was involved in the foundation of the Prison Fellowship in Northern Ireland, Scotland, Canada, New Zealand and Australia. She is the wife of Conservative MP Michael Alison.

Florence Allshorn 1887–1950

Florence Allshorn served as a missionary in Uganda. On her return she spent 12 years training missionaries for CMS in the UK. She founded the St Julian's Community as a place of restoration and further study for missionaries on home-leave.

Gladys Aylward 1902–70

Born in North London, Gladys Aylward left school at 14 to become a parlourmaid but overcame all obstacles to realize her dream of becoming a missionary in China. She worked there for 20 years and then, when war with Japan resulted in bombing of the area where she lived, she led 100 homeless children on a 12-day trek over the mountains to safety. Her story is told in *The Small Woman* by Alan Burgess, and the film, *The Inn of the Sixth Happiness*, which starred Ingrid Bergman. After returning to England for a number of years, Gladys Aylward settled in Taiwan in 1953 as head of an orphanage.

Olave, Lady Baden-Powell CBE 1889–1977

Lady Baden-Powell was born in England in 1889. At the age of 23 she became engaged to the 55-year-old founder of the Boy Scouts, and lived to found the Girl Guides, travel the world both with her husband and after his death, alone, to continue his work.

Melody Beattie

Melody Beattie is an American writer, born in 1949, who has liberated countless troubled and damaged people through her books on co-dependency and bereavement.

Lin Berwick

Lin Berwick, is a multiple-disabled young woman who has cerebral palsy and is blind, and wheelchair-bound most of the time. She is an author, counsellor and Methodist Lay Preacher.

Julie Billiart 1751–1816

Julie Billiart is a most attractive character. A down-to-earth peasant woman of enormous faith, humour and stamina, she opened schools in nine places in France and eleven in Belgium, founding the Sisters of Notre Dame to teach and care for the pupils.

Elizabeth Blackwell 1821–1910

Elizabeth Blackwell, an American, was the first woman to qualify as a medical doctor (1849). Deeply religious, she devoted her life to work among the poorest of women and children in New York and after much opposition, founded a hospital for training women medical students, which opened on Florence Nightingale's birthday.

Margaret Blagge 1652–77

Margaret Blagge was a Restoration beauty, who, because her father had a position at court, was at 16 a lady-in-waiting at the court of Charles I. Devout and pious, she was also a talented actress and a general favourite, whose diary reveals how she strove to live a Christian life in a very worldly, dissolute environment. She married the Earl of Godolphin and was bliss-fully happy in her marriage, which ended with her death in childbirth at the age of 25.

Margaret Bondfield 1873–1953

Somerset-born, Margaret Bondfield's trade union work led her into Labour politics. She was chairman of the TUC in 1923 and the first woman cabinet minister as Minister of Labour between 1929 and 1931.

Catherine Booth 1829–90

Catherine Booth is famous as the 'mother' of the Salvation Army. With her husband, William, she started the Church Mission in London in 1865, which became known as the Salvation Army in 1878. She realized that the outcasts they sought to help would never be found in churches or chapels, but had to be met in their own hovels. Her talent as a preacher, and the novelty at that time of hearing a woman preach, provided much interest and funding for the work, and she was strongly supported in this by her husband. The Salvation Army was very much a joint venture.

Maria Boulding
Maria Boulding is a contemplative nun at Stanbrook Abbey and the author of several books.

Josephine Butler 1828–1906
Josephine Butler was born into a privileged and sheltered English family, a branch of Lord Grey's of Reform Bill fame. Witty, beautiful and highly intelligent, she always had a deep concern for the sufferings of others, and was especially the champion of the exploited. She married George Butler who became headmaster of Cheltenham College and then principal of Liverpool College. It was in Liverpool that Josephine came into contact with prostitutes whose welfare became her major concern, shocking polite society of the day with its double standards. A prominent Anglican lay woman, she was a lifelong campaigner for women's rights and suffrage.

Joan Porter Buxton
Joan Porter Buxton was adopted into an upper-class family in the Edwardian era, after the early death of her father in Egypt. Her book, *You've Got to Take a Chance!* tells the story of her difficult early years and of how she came to terms with the loss of identity and confusion resulting from being told rather cruelly, at the age of twelve, that she was adopted. Her story continues with the re-discovery of her mother, her coming to faith, and final years of reconciliation and happiness.

Amy Carmichael 1868–1951
Amy Carmichael was born in Northern Ireland and founded the Dohnavur Fellowship in South India which rescued children sold into Hindu temple service. She wrote many books and poems despite much ill-health in later years.

Clare of Assisi c.1194–1253
Clare of Assisi was a native of Assisi who was inspired by God and the example of Francis to found monasteries of sisters in Italy, France and Germany.

Kate Compston
Kate Compston is a minister of the United Reformed Church, based in Hampshire, and a writer of prayers, poems and meditations.

Elizabeth L. Comstock 1815–90

Elizabeth Comstock was an English member of the Society of Friends. She travelled to America where Abraham Lincoln arranged for her free access to all hospitals. There she worked with the wounded of both armies during the Civil War, and with soldiers in army prisons, as well as with negroes.

Margaret Cundiff

Margaret Cundiff was born in Somerset but has lived in the north of England since early childhood. Since 1973 she has served on the staff of St James' Church, Selby, North Yorkshire, and was ordained deacon in 1987, and later priest. She is a popular writer and broadcaster.

Mary Endersbee

Mary Endersbee was born in Cheshire, England, and worked in a bank before becoming Assistant Editor of *Crusade* magazine after recovering from a nervous breakdown.

Kathleen Ferrier 1912–53

One of the world's finest opera singers, Kathleen Ferrier was born in Lancashire, England. After winning a prize for singing in a local music festival she began serious studies in 1940. Her rich contralto voice and wide range won her a great reputation and many recordings exist of her fine performances.

Betty Ford

Betty Ford may be known most publicly as the wife of former President of the United States, Gerald Ford, but her place in this book comes from her own courage and religious faith, drawn on during her battle with drug addiction and alcoholism. The Betty Ford Center in Palm Springs has brought hope and recovery to many.

Elizabeth Fry 1780–1845

Elizabeth Fry was the great Quaker prison reformer. Born in Norwich, she had eleven children and after teaching and founding a school for children, felt she was still doing little useful with her life! In 1813 she was taken to see Newgate Prison by a visiting American Quaker and was so horrified by the appalling conditions of the women prisoners that she dedicated herself to helping them. Practical actions such as providing decent clothes and teaching them to teach their children, helped restore their self-respect. She even organized support groups of prisoners to help them prepare for and endure being transported overseas for their crimes. To give them comfort and moral support, she accompanied the women to every convict ship that left London for nearly 20 years until she died.

The Grail Society
The Grail Society was the first Secular Institute to be recognized in England. It is a women's group which has its central house in North London.

Valerie Hadert
Valerie Hadert has Multiple Sclerosis. She is now a permanent patient in a hospital near London, takes a lively interest in her local church and writes verse, some of which has been published in *Challenge and Decision*, and used as the basis of songs by Cliff Richard.

Margaret Hebblethwaite
Margaret Hebblethwaite was born in London in 1951. She read theology and philosophy at Oxford and studied spirituality at the Gregorian University, Rome. Her book, *Motherhood and God,* marries her theological training with her own experience as a mother of two small, lively children.

Margaret K. Henrichsen
Margaret Henrichsen's book, *Seven Steeples*, tells of her life as minister of seven churches in New England. After the death of her husband, she struggled for five years to study for the ministry and ordination.

Margaret Holden
Margaret Holden was arrested for sharing in a vigil of silent prayer on the steps of the Ministry of Defence, Whitehall, London.

Caryll Houselander 1901–54
Caryll Houselander was a prolific Roman Catholic writer of prose and poetry. Her biographer, Maisie Sheed, wrote:'her books sold like novels... not offering help to her readers as the fruit of her own victory but inviting them to join her in a battle that she was fighting to the very end of her life... It was from conscious weakness not from strength that she brought to others the power of God's love.'

Elizabeth Fox Howard 1873–1957
Elizabeth Fox Howard came from an old Quaker family but only became a member of the Society of Friends when she was 30. She was active in

various humanitarian causes, and during the 1914–18 war she was the visiting Quaker chaplain to conscientious objectors in prison, and also worked on behalf of 'enemy aliens'.

Julian of Norwich 1342–1415

Julian of Norwich was a contemporary of Chaucer and perhaps the only Englishwoman generally accepted as a great mystic of the medieval church. During a near-fatal illness in 1373, she received 16 visions which she carefully recorded. Over the following years, she meditated on them and produced a revised and expanded version 20 years later, entitled *The Revelations of Divine Love*. Despite her determined attempt to be a self-effacing author, her writings reveal a cheerful, devout and straightforward personality. She lived as an anchoress in a small cottage or cell attached to the wall of St Julian's Church in Norfolk, where she received visitors who came to her window and provided them with good advice.

Victoria Lidiard

Victoria Lidiard was born in England in 1889 and was active in the Women's Social and Political Union, a suffragette organization. Trained as an optician, she was the first woman on the honorary staff of the London Refraction Hospital. A first committee member of the Anglican Welfare of Animals Society, she was active in many animal welfare organizations.

Catherine Marshall

Catherine Marshall is a well-known American writer. After her first husband, Peter Marshall, died leaving her a young widow with two young children, she wrote his life story in *A Man Called Peter*. Later books chronicled her life of faith, her work and her subsequent remarriage and family life.

Mechthild of Magdeburg 1210–82

Mechthild of Magdeburg was a German mystic who lived a hermit-like existence, writing down her visions and revelations for around 20 years before becoming a Cistercian nun.

Hannah More 1745–1833

Hannah More was an Anglican religious writer and philanthropist, a friend of Dr Johnson, the actor David Garrick, William Wilberforce and John Newton the hymnwriter. Her plays found great success on the London stage but after moving to Somerset, she committed herself to providing schools for the mining villages of the Mendips and friendly Societies to relieve the poverty and hardship she discovered there. Her writings were aimed at the wealthy classes to stir their conscience and the poorer ordinary folk via the lively Cheap Repository Tracts which she wrote and published.

Janet Morley

Janet Morley is an Adult Education Adviser at Christian Aid, a writer and editor who has significantly contributed to the cause of women's ministry in the Church of England.

Florence Nightingale 1820–1910

Florence Nightingale was a famous English hospital reformer. She began her training as a nurse in 1851 and served exhaustively abroad during the Crimean War. A superb administrator, her practical talents were balanced and nourished by her deep religious faith. The strong mystical leanings she felt always had to be translated into appropriate action.

Anne Ortlund

Anne Ortlund is an American writer of Christian books on faith, the family and the life of the Christian woman. Married to a pastor, she has three adult children.

Barbara Piller

Barbara Piller, formerly Mrs Barbara Clayton, was a nurse in Rwanda with CMS. A few weeks after giving birth to her daughter, she spent her first wedding anniversary a widow. Her husband, John Clayton, was shot by Rwandan refugees who had been persuaded to rob them.

Eugenia Price

Eugenia Price was a successful American television producer when she became a Christian at the age of 33. From that moment she began an outstanding ministry of writing and broadcasting.

Joan Puls OSF

Joan Puls OSF is an American Franciscan. She lives in an ecumenical community in Norfolk and conducts retreats. She has written and co-written a number of books.

Helen Roseveare

Helen Roseveare was a medical missionary with WEC International. A doctor who spent 20 years in the Congo (now Zaire), she was held in captivity for five months during the revolution in 1964.

Sue Ryder, Lady Rider of Warsaw CMG, OBE

Sue Ryder is an English philanthropist and promoter of residential care for the sick and disabled. She joined the First Nursing Yeomanry during the Second World War and later served with the Polish section of the Special Operations Executive, working for part of the time in occupied Europe. Her experiences provided the vision of creating a 'living memorial' to those who died and those who, like refugees, continued to suffer as a result of the war. She established the Sue Ryder Foundation in 1953. In 1959 she married Leonard Cheshire.

May Sarton

May Sarton is the American author of several much-loved and popular journals, including those chronicling her life and struggles in old age and following a stroke. She is also an internationally acclaimed poet and novelist.

Dame Cicely Saunders

Dame Cicely Saunders is the English pioneer of the modern hospice movement, contributing research, teaching a new approach to caring, particularly for families. She trained at St Thomas' Hospital Medical School and the Nightingale School of Nursing. She founded St Christopher's Hospice in Sydenham in 1967 to promote the principles of dying with dignity.

Dorothy L. Sayers 1893–1957

Dorothy Sayers is an Englishwoman who wrote detective stories featuring aristocratic detective Lord Peter Wimsey. After University, she worked for about ten years as a copywriter for an advertising agency, during which time she wrote most of her detective fiction. Her reputation as a Christian apologist and playwright is crowned by the series *The Man Born to be King*, which was broadcast by the BBC in 1941–42. At the time, the portrayal of the character of Jesus and the use of everyday, colloquial language stirred up quite a controversy!

Aida Skripnikova

Aida Skripnikova was arrested for distributing hand-printed Gospel tracts in Leningrad and spent a number of years in prison for her faith. She suffered the loss of her job as a lab assistant and was forced to work on a building site. After various arrests and trials, and brief forced detention in a psychiatric clinic, she was sentenced to three years' imprisonment in 1968.

Hannah Whitall Smith

Hannah Whitall Smith wrote one of America's classic inspirational books: *The Christian's Secret of a Happy Life*. Born into a Quaker family, she was a founder member of the Women's Christian Movement and the suffrage movement in the USA.

JoAnn Kelley Smith

JoAnn Kelley Smith described herself as 'A Dying Person' in the period during which she and her family coped with the terminal cancer which finally took her life on Friday, 25th October 1974.

Dorothee Soelle

Dorothee Soelle is a theologian and author, born in Cologne and now living in Hamburg.

Elizabeth Stuart

Elizabeth Stuart was born in 1963, in Gravesend, Kent, England, to an Anglican father and a Catholic mother. She read theology at Oxford and now lectures in theology at the College of St Mark and St John, Plymouth.

Hettie Taylor

Hettie Taylor was teacher at the school in Aberfan, Wales, which was crushed by slippage of the spoil heaps from the local mines. She was there on the day when 144 people were killed, including 116 children.

Corrie ten Boom 1892–1983

Corrie ten Boom was the daughter of a Dutch watchmaker when Germany invaded Holland. She became involved in the work to enable persecuted Jews to escape, and as a result she was imprisoned in the concentration camp at Ravensbruck where her sister died. Out of her sufferings came a ministry of hope and reconciliation, as she preached and wrote widely.

Mother Teresa

Mother Teresa was born in 1910, Agnes Gouxha Bejaxhu, to Albanian peasant parents living in Yugoslavia. She became a nun in 1927 and was sent to Dublin in 1928. But India was her particular concern, and she spent 20 years teaching in Calcutta before the call came to serve the people of the slums. 'The biggest disease today is not leprosy or tuberculosis, but rather the feeling of being unwanted, uncared for, deserted by everybody.' In 1950 she opened the Mother House of the Missionary Sisters of Charity and in 1970 a novitiate for Europeans and Americans. She was awarded the Nobel Peace Prize for her work.

Evelyn Underhill 1875–1941

Evelyn Underhill was an Anglican lay woman who wrote extensively about mysticism and the spiritual life. She acted as a spiritual director and also led retreats. Her work emphasizes the importance of training and discipline, and that contemplation should always lead to action.

Pauline Webb

Pauline Webb is a broadcaster and writer. Born in north-east London, she has travelled extensively. Former Vice-President of the Methodist Conference, she was Vice-Moderator of the World Council of Churches from 1968 until 1975. A Fellow of King's College, London, she holds degrees from London University and Union Theological Seminary, New York, with honorary doctorates from universities in Brussels, Toronto and Halifax, Nova Scotia.

Index of Authors

Index of Sources

Sylvia Mary Alison, *God is Building a House*, Marshall Morgan & Scott, 1984

Florence Allshorn in *URC Prayer Handbook,* 1987

Regis J. Armstrong OFM and Ignatius Brady OFM (translation and introduction), *Francis and Clare: The Complete Works*, SPCK, 1982

Olave, Lady Baden Powell, as told to Mary Drewery, *Window on My Heart*, Hodder & Stoughton, 1973

Marion Beales, 'News Share', Congregational Federation, in *URC Prayer Handbook,* 1995

Melody Beattie, *Codependents' Guide to the Twelve Steps*, Judy Piatkus, 1991

Lin Berwick, *Inner Vision*, Arthur James Ltd, 1990

Elizabeth Blackwell, *Pioneer Work in Opening the Medical Profession to Women*, London, 1895

Maude Blanford in Catherine Marshall, *Claiming God's Promises*, Hodder & Stoughton, 1973

Margaret Bondfield, *What Life Has Taught Me*, Odhams

Catherine Booth, *Female Ministry*, Salvation Army Book Dept, 1909

Maria Boulding, *Gateway to Hope*, Fount, 1985

Josephine Butler, *Personal Reminiscences of a Great Crusade*, London, 1896

Joan Porter Buxton, *You've Got to Take a Chance!* Grosvenor Books, undated

Lavinia Byrne, *The Hidden Tradition*, SPCK, 1993

Amy Carmichael, *Candles in the Dark*, Triangle, SPCK, 1981

Gwen Cashmore and Joan Puls OSF, *Clearing the Way*, World Council of Churches, Geneva

Clergyman's widow in R. Blythe, *The View in Winter*, Allen Lane, 1979

Jeremy and Margaret Collingwood, *Hannah More*, Lion, 1990

Kate Compston in *URC Prayer Handbook,* 1993 and 1995

Elizabeth L. Comstock, *Life and Letters of Elizabeth L. Comstock*, Headley, 1895

Mary Craig, *Blessings*, Hodder & Stoughton, 1979

Margaret Cundiff, *Travelling Light*, Triangle, SPCK, 1992

Mary Endersbee (ed.), *Taught by Pain*, Falcon Books, Church Pastoral Aid Society, 1972

John Evelyn, *Life of Mrs Godolphin*, Pickering, 1847

Betty Ford with Chris Chase, *Betty: A Glad Awakening*, Jove/Doubleday, 1988

Elizabeth Fry, *Observations on the Visiting, Superintending and Government of Female Prisoners*, London, 1827

The Grail Society in Olive Wyon, *Living Springs*, SCM Press, 1963

Valerie Hadert in Mary Endersbee (ed.), *Taught by Pain,* Falcon Books, Church Pastoral Aid Society, 1972

Margaret Hebblethwaite, *Motherhood and God*, Geoffrey Chapman, 1984

Margaret K. Henrichsen, *Seven Steeples: A Minister and her People*, Harper & Row, 1967

Enid Henke in Dame Cicely Saunders, *Beyond the Horizon,* Darton, Longman & Todd, 1989

Josephine Hilton in Catherine Marshall, *Claiming God's Promises,* Hodder & Stoughton, 1973

Margaret Holden in *URC Prayer Handbook*, 1989

Elizabeth Fox Howard from a letter published in *The Friend* by The Society of Friends and in Elfrida Vipont, *The High Way*; *Midstream, A Record of Many Years*, 1949

Xenia Howard-Johnston and Michael Bourdeaux (eds), *Aida of Leningrad*, Gateway Outreach, 1972

Bishop Penny Jamieson, Dunedin, New Zealand, 1995

Julian of Norwich in *URC Prayer Handbook*, 1987

Victoria Lidiard, *Christianity: Faith, Love and Healing*, Vantage Press, 1985

Sister Mary Linscott SND, *To Heaven on Foot* (about St Julie Billiart)

Kate McIlhagga in *URC Prayer Handbook,* 1995

Catherine Marshall, *Claiming God's Promises*, Hodder & Stoughton, 1973; *Meeting God at Every Turn*, Hodder & Stoughton, 1981

Mechthild of Magdeburg in Lucy Menzies, *Mirror of the Holy*, Mowbray, 1928

S.B. Meech (ed.) *The Book of Margery Kempe 1436*, 1940

Katherine Moore, *She for God*, Allison & Busby, 1978

Hannah More, *The Spirit of Prayer*; *Turn the Carpet*, Cheap Repository Tract; *Strictures on the Modern System of Education with a View of the Principles and Conduct Prevalent among Women of Rank and Fortune*, Volume II, 1799

Janet Morley (ed.), *Bread of Tomorrow*, SPCK/Christian Aid, 1993

J.H. Oldham, *Florence Allshorn and the Story of St Julian's*, SCM Press, 1956

Anne Ortlund, *Disciplines of the Beautiful Woman*, Word Incorporated, 1977, 1989

Barbara Piller in Mary Endersbee (ed.), *Taught by Pain,* Falcon Books, Church Pastoral Aid Society, 1972

Eugenia Price, *A Woman's Choice*, Oliphant, 1962; *The Burden is Light*, Jove/Doubleday, 1985

Joan Puls OSF, *Every Bush is Burning*, WCC, 1985

Rosalind Rinker, *You Can Witness with Confidence*, Zondervan

Helen Roseveare, *Living Faith*, Hodder & Stoughton, 1980

Baroness Ryder of Warsaw, *Child of My Love*, Collins Harvill, 1986

May Sarton, *Journal of a Solitude*, The Women's Press, 1994; *Encore: A Journal of the Eightieth Year*, The Women's Press, 1993

Dame Cicely Saunders (ed.), *Beyond the Horizon*, Darton, Longman and Todd, 1990

Dorothy L. Sayers, *Creed or Chaos*, Methuen

A Sister from Buikidnon in *URC Prayer Handbook*, 1995

Cecil Woodham Smith, *Life of Florence Nightingale*, 1950

Hannah Whitall Smith, *The Christian's Secret of a Happy Life*, Spire, 1968

JoAnn Kelley Smith, *Free Fall*, SPCK, 1977

Mary F. Smith, *A Sacramental Approach to Modern Life*, The Society of Friends

Dorothee Soelle (translated by Joyce Irwin), *Celebrating Resistance*, Mowbray, 1993

Margaret Spufford in *URC Prayer Handbook*, 1988; *Celebration*, Fount

Elizabeth Stuart, *Through Brokenness*, Fount, 1990

Karen Summers, Vancouver School of Theology, 1987 in Pauline Webb, *Candles for Advent*, Fount, 1989

Hettie Taylor in Catherine Marshall, *Claiming God's Promises*, Hodder & Stoughton, 1973

Corrie ten Boom, *Amazing Love*, Christian Literature Crusade/ Kingsway, 1953

Mother Teresa in URC *Prayer Handbook*, 1989

Evelyn Underhill in Elfrida Vipont (ed.), *The High Way*, Oxford University Press, 1957

Elizabeth Gray Vining, *The World in Tune*, Harper & Bros, NY

Elfrida Vipont (ed.), *The High Way*, Oxford University Press, 1957

Maisie Ward, *Caryll Houselander*, Sheed & Ward, 1962

Pauline Webb, *Candles for Advent*, Fount, 1989

Katie Whitelegg, *Faith was my Only Companion*, Curlew Press, undated

Märta Wilhelmsson, from *No Longer Strangers*, WCC, Geneva

Charles Williams (ed.), *Letters of Evelyn Underhill*, London, 1943

Lois Wilson, *Women in a Changing World*, World Council of Churches

Index of Subjects

153

Acknowledgments

We would like to thank all those who have given us permission to include material in this book, as indicated below. Every effort has been made to trace and contact copyright owners. If there are any inadvertent omissions or errors in the acknowledgments, we apologize to those concerned and will remedy them in the next edition. Each figure refers to the page number of the extract.

Sylvia Mary Alison: from *God is Building a House*, Marshall Morgan & Scott, 1984: 89.

Gladys Aylward: from *Claiming God's Promises*, ed. Catherine Marshall, Hodder & Stoughton, 1973: 121.

Olave, Lady Baden-Powell: from Mary Drewery, *Window on my Heart*, copyright © 1973 by Lady Baden-Powell and Mary Drewery. Reproduced by permission of Hodder & Stoughton Ltd: 127

Melody Beattie: extract from *Codependents' Guide to the Twelve Steps*, published by Piatkus Books and Simon and Schuster: 129, 130.

Maude Blanford: from *Claiming God's Promises*, ed. Catherine Marshall, Hodder & Stoughton, 1973: 54.

Margaret Bondfield: from *What Life Has Taught Me*, Odhams: 28. From *Candles in the Dark* by Amy Carmichael. Copyright © 1981 The Dohnavur Fellowship, London: 1982 Christian Literature Crusade, Ft. Washington. Used by permission: 52.

Gwen Cashmore: from *Clearing the Way* by Gwen Cashmore and Joan Puls OSF, WCC Publications, World Council of Churches, Geneva, Switzerland. Used with permission: 75.

Cassell plc: from Margaret Hebblethwaite, *Motherhood and God*, Geoffrey Chapman, 1984: 37, 43, 51, 69, 95, 121, 122, 125; from Lucy Menzies, *Mirror of the Holy*, Mowbray, 1928, for Mechthild of Magdeburg: 19; from Dorothee Soelle (tr. Joyce Irwin), *Celebrating Resistance*, Mowbray, 1993: 110.

Christian Aid/SPCK: from *Bread of Tomorrow*, Janet Morley: 108.

Clergyman's widow: from *The View in Winter*, Allen Lane, 1979. Copyright © Ronald Blythe, 1979. Reproduced by permission of the author c/o Rogers, Coleridge & White Ltd., 20 Powis Mews, London W11 1JN: 59.

Kate Compston: from *Encompassing Presence, the Prayer Handbook, 1993* and *A Restless Hope, the Prayer Handbook, 1995*, published by the United Reformed Church: 22, 102

The Congregational Federation: from Marion Beales, 'News Share', published in *A Restless Hope, the Prayer Handbook, 1995*: 117.

Mary Craig: *Blessings*. Copyright © 1979 by Mary Craig. Reproduced by permission of Hodder & Stoughton Ltd: 70.

Mary Endersbee: from *Taught by Pain*, Falcon Books, 1972: 46.

Kathleen Ferrier: from *A Woman's Choice* by Eugenia Price, Oliphants, 1962: 72.

Betty Ford: from *Betty: A Glad Awakening* by Betty Ford with Chris Chase, Jove/Doubleday, 1988: 17, 50, 56, 105.

The Grail Publications: from The Grail Society: 99.

Grosvenor Books: from Joan Porter Buxton, *You've Got to Take a Chance!*: 21, 57, 60, 66, 128.

Valerie Hadert: from *Taught by Pain*, ed. Mary Endersbee, Falcon Books, 1972: 71.

HarperCollins Publishers: from *Gateway to Hope*, Maria Boulding: 39; from *Child of My Love*, Sue Ryder: 83; from *Celebration*, Margaret Spufford: 72, 74; from *Through Brokenness*, Elizabeth Stuart: 17, 18, 37, 38, 42, 84, 123, 124; from *Candles for Advent*, Pauline Webb: 73, 115, 127.

Margaret K. Henrichsen, from *Seven Steeples: A Minister and Her People*, Harper & Row: 27.

Enid Henke: from *Beyond the Horizon*, ed. Dame Cicely Saunders, Darton, Longman and Todd, 1989: 64.

Josephine Hilton: from *Claiming God's Promises*, ed. Catherine Marshall, Hodder & Stoughton, 1973: 68.

R.A. Hodgkin: from Mary F. Smith, *A Sacramental Approach to Modern Life*, published by the Society of Friends: 36, 109.

Margaret Holden: from *All the Glorious Names, the Prayer Handbook 1989*, published by the United Reformed Church: 103.

Michael Howard: from Elizabeth Fox Howard: 80, 135.

Arthur James: from Lin Berwick, *Inner Vision*, Arthur James Ltd, 1990: 38, 67.

Keston Institute: from *Aida of Leningrad*, eds Xenia Howard-Johnston and Michael Bourdeaux, Gateway Outreach: Aida Skripnikova: 53, 87, 109.

Kingsway Communications: from Corrie ten Boom, *Amazing Love*: 67, 88, 96.

Victoria Lidiard: from *Christianity: Faith, Love and Healing*, Vantage Press, 1985: 20.

Catherine Marshall: from *Meeting God at Every Turn*. Reproduced by permission of Hodder & Stoughton Ltd (copyright © 1981), and Chosen Books, USA: 49. From *Claiming God's Promises* by Catherine Marshall and others, Hodder & Stoughton, 1981: 26, 54.

Kate McIlhagga: from *Encompassing Presence, the Prayer Handbook, 1995*, published by the United Reformed Church: 82.

Nelson Word UK: from *Disciplines of the Beautiful Woman*, Anne Ortlund: 30, 55.

Barbara Piller: from *Taught by Pain*, ed. Mary Endersbee, Falcon Books, 1972: 44.

Eugenia Price: from *A Woman's Choice*, Oliphants, 1962: 31, 51, 96, 124, 125. From *The Burden is Light*, Jove/Doubleday, 1965: 23, 25.

Joan Puls OSF: from *Clearing the Way* by Gwen Cashmore and Joan Puls OSF, WCC Publications, World Council of Churches, Geneva, Switzerland. Used with permission: 75. From *Every Bush is Burning* (copyright © 1985), WCC Publications, World Council of Churches, Geneva, Switzerland. Used with permission: 88.

Rosalind Rinker: from *You Can Witness With Confidence*, Zondervan Publishing House: 114.

Helen Roseveare: from *Living Faith*, Hodder & Stoughton, 1980: 100, 131.

May Sarton: from *Journal of a Solitude*. Copyright © 1973 by May Sarton. Reprinted by permission of W.W. Norton & Company, Inc. From *Encore: A Journal of the Eightieth Year* by May Sarton. Copyright © 1993 by May Sarton. Reprinted by permission of W.W. Norton & Company, Inc. The extracts from *Journal of a Solitude* and *Encore: A Journal of the Eightieth Year* by May Sarton: published in Great Britain by The Women's Press Ltd, 1985 and 1993 respectively, 34 Great Sutton Street, London EC1V 0DX, are used by permission of The Women's Press Ltd: 16, 120.

Darton, Longman and Todd: from *Beyond the Horizon*, Dame Cicely Saunders: 64, 70.

Dorothy L. Sayers: from *Creed or Chaos*, Methuen: 81.

SCM Press: from J.H. Oldham, *Florence Allshorn*: 22, 30, 57, 61, 77, 86, 87, 95, 97, 112, 116, 123.

Sister from Buikidnon: from *A Restless Hope, the Prayer Handbook 1995*, published by the United Reformed Church: 114.

Sheed & Ward: from Maisie Ward, *Caryll Houselander*: 16, 24, 25, 32, 33, 45, 48, 50, 60, 62, 63, 68, 75, 83, 97, 105, 106, 130.

The Sisters of Notre Dame: from Mary Linscott SND, *To Heaven on Foot*, Julie Billiart: 17, 18, 23, 80, 96.

SPCK: from *Francis and Clare: the Complete Works*, 1982, trs and intro by Regis J. Armstrong OFM Cap and Ignatius Brady OFM, for Clare of Assisi: 92; from Margaret Cundiff: *Travelling Light through St Mark's Gospel*, Triangle, 1992: 24, 33, 34, 36, 43, 58, 76, 84, 104, 107; from JoAnn Kelley Smith, *Free Fall*, 1977: 42, 47, 61, 62, 76.

Hannah Whitall Smith: from *The Christian's Secret of a Happy Life*, Spire, 1968. Copyright © 1942 by the Fleming H. Revell Company: 34.

Karen Summer: from *Candles for Advent* by Pauline Webb, Fount/HarperCollins Publishers, 1989: 126.

Hettie Taylor: from *Claiming God's Promises*, with John and Elizabeth Sherrill, ed. Catherine Marshall, Hodder & Stoughton, 1973: 74.

Mother Teresa: from *All the Glorious Names, the Prayer Handbook 1989*, published by the United Reformed Church: 83.

Elizabeth Gray Vining: from *The World in Tune*, Harper & Bros, NY: 98.

Katie Whitelegg: from *Faith was My Only Companion*, Curlew Press: 131.

Marta Wilhelmsson: from *No Longer Strangers*, WCC Publications, World Council of Churches, Geneva, Switzerland. Used with permission: 113.

Lois Wilson: from *Women in a Changing World*, WCC Publications, World Council of Churches, Geneva, Switzerland. Used with permission: 113.